Double Exposure

Double Exposure

*How Social Psychology Fell in
Love with the Movies*

KATHRYN MILLARD

RUTGERS UNIVERSITY PRESS
NEW BRUNSWICK, CAMDEN, AND NEWARK,
NEW JERSEY, AND LONDON

LCCN 2021023671

A British Cataloging-in-Publication record for this book is available from the British Library.

References to internet websites (URLs) were accurate at the time of writing. Neither the author nor Rutgers University Press is responsible for URLs that may have expired or changed since the manuscript was prepared.

♾ The paper used in this publication meets the requirements of the American National Standard for Information Sciences—Permanence of Paper for Printed Library Materials, ANSI Z39.48-1992.

www.rutgersuniversitypress.org

Manufactured in the United States of America

Contents

Double Exposure

Introduction

Double Exposure examines the role of cinema and moving images in shaping social psychology's key postwar experiments. As a writer, filmmaker, and interdisciplinary scholar, I have a long-standing interest in such experiments and the films claimed as evidence of their findings. We are told that most of us will inflict electric shocks on a fellow citizen if ordered to—acting as a brutal prison guard once we put on a uniform. We will walk on by when we see a stranger in need of help. These are the most commonly shared stories from Stanley Milgram's "Obedience to Authority" (1963), Philip Zimbardo's "Stanford Prison Experiment" (1971), and John M. Darley and Bibb Latané's "Bystander Effect" (1968)—the social psychology experiments I think of as the Big Three.

When I was twenty, I worked briefly in a juvenile detention center for kids in trouble with the law. After a riot made local headlines, I was one of several community workers brought in to be "new brooms." The minimum age rule was waived on my account. I was motivated by a mix of idealism and pragmatism— I hoped to change some kids' lives for the better. Additionally, I needed the money, since the first community worker jobs I took were unpaid. Footage of Milgram's documentary *Obedience* (1965) and Zimbardo's "Stanford Prison Experiment" featured in the boot camp–style induction. Or did they? I recall the experiments being discussed in our training. I recall being taken to a prison cell and shut inside. The thinking behind this was that the experience would help us identify with our juvenile charges. If that was indeed the rationale, it worked only too well in my case. I began to feel that I was serving time myself. In fact, so ill-suited was I to the position of jailer that I was soon let go. I became a community media worker, then an independent filmmaker, completed postgraduate work in history and film, and became a university professor of screen.

Why do we tell stories about groups that emphasize compliance and obedience rather than independence and cooperation? The familiar narratives form

1

only half the picture. There is considerable evidence that most people refuse to harm others—that we do not routinely identify with assigned roles—that strangers find ways to work together during crises. Surprisingly, new evidence alone has not been sufficient to shift the story. As individuals and communities, we are the stories we tell. However, we are also the stories that we have the narrative resources to tell.

The most influential social psychology experiments left a trail of visual evidence. In writing *Double Exposure*, I aimed to examine these experiments through the lens of a filmmaker. By focusing on this set of films, I aimed to provide a revisionist account of the experiments themselves, the documentaries that investigators claimed as evidence, and the subsequent cinematic retelling of these events. Over time, these visual narratives have become fixed in cultural memory.

Wherever I first saw them, the compelling black-and-white images of *Obedience* and stills of Zimbardo's prison simulation stayed with me. They are now firmly, irrevocably associated with an earlier period of my life. Double exposure is the second exposure of an already exposed piece of film. Like this double exposure, my memories are layered one on top of the other.

In 2013, I was invited to speak on the topic "Milgram as a Filmmaker" at the "Legacy of Stanley Milgram Conference" at Yale Law School. My fellow speakers were drawn primarily from psychology and the law. I noted how much of our respective work combined insights from different fields—not only social psychology and legal studies but also mind sciences, economics, sociology, criminology, history, biography, and, in my case, drama and film. As is widely acknowledged, innovation often occurs in the spaces between disciplines rather than from the center of established fields. Therefore, the sources I have drawn on in this book are necessarily eclectic.

"Stanley Milgram as Filmmaker": this was the title of my project for my very first request to the Milgram Archives at Yale in 2008. I have now been researching films of social psychology experiments for close to fifteen years. Initially, I was deeply attracted to the notion that film could flush out new insights into human behavior—although I was somewhat skeptical about the notion of proof. Did their images really provide the evidence that psychology experimenters claimed? Milgram called his "Obedience to Authority" studies a "laboratory drama." Could a film double as art and science, drama and experiment? Attempting to answer these questions, I have undertaken extensive archival research, read across the vast literature devoted to these experiments within psychology and the social sciences, and made three documentaries in collaboration with social psychologists: *Shock Room* (2015), *Experiment 20* (2018), and *The Bystander Story* (2021; in postproduction at the time of writing).

Not long after I moved to Sydney as a young adult, my detective father visited me from interstate. Perhaps this is etched in my memory because he died a year or so later. I remember we had dinner at his hotel, across the road from the shabbily elegant Central Station. Not so practiced at holidays, my father seemed ill at ease off duty. He lived for what the cops of his era called "The Job." On leaving the hotel restaurant, I headed for Central Station and caught a train home. I unlocked the front door and went into the kitchen. The phone rang—it was my father. He had watched me from the hotel window; crossing the road, I had not gone directly to Central Station. Instead, I had gone from A to B, from B to D, D to F, and only then to C. "This was dangerous," he said—there were murderers on the streets of Sydney. (To be fair, a particularly vicious abduction, rape, and murder case had been featured recently on the national news.) I cannot recall my exact reply—I said something about the particular configuration of crossings and traffic lights—regardless, my father was adamant: "Always take the most direct path."

As I researched this project, I found myself recalling my father's tips on pursuing inquiries; I have not always taken the most direct path, choosing instead to examine the topic from different vantage points. I gradually became aware that crime scenes—from the Good Samaritan's road to Jericho, city streets, and dimly lit laboratories in university basements—were integral to the dramaturgy of social psychology's landmark experiments. Writing about detective stories, Stefano Tani observed that "a discovery is not about finding something new, but rather, about finding a missing link."[1]

When I begin a new film project, I write myself a brief—a set of guiding principles, if you like. I did the same for *Double Exposure*:

- History is a double investigation. Ivan Jablonka advocated history as a double investigation:[2] a form of inquiry in which the researcher's involvement, subjectivity, and point of view are all clear. After all, "researchers are tied to the object of their work by thousands of invisible threads."[3] Exactly.
- Look for patterns. When immersed in any ongoing inquiry, it can be difficult to see the big picture. According to criminal investigators, one should "seize on patterns that lie just below the surface of recognition."[4]
- Literature of fact. "To create the literature of fact, we select," wrote historian Timothy Garton Ash: "we cast light on this object, shadow on that."[5] Another term for this is the "literature of the real."[6]
- Follow the richest vein of evidence. Robert Darnton, historian and journalist, has an astonishing ability to find the telling detail among a wealth of archival material. How? "I have followed what seemed to be the richest run of documents," he wrote, "following leads wherever they went and quickening my pace as soon as I stumbled on a surprise."[7]
- As a form, the essay aims to ask questions and probe and test ideas. "Thought does not advance in a single direction; rather, aspects of the argument interweave as in a carpet."[8] *Double Exposure* tilts towards the essay—partly due to the fact that this book is aimed at more than one readership: academics in film and social psychology as well as general readers.

Chapter 1 sketches the early relationship between cinema and psychology. The latter emerged as a distinct discipline at approximately the same time as the invention of cinema in the late nineteenth century. Investigators soon swapped diaries for cameras. In the process, the boundaries between art and science, documentation and entertainment were often blurred. The chapter considers how the films of Frank and Lillian Gilbreth, Hugo Münsterberg, Arnold Gessler, Kurt Lewin, Alan Funt, and others prepared the way for postwar experiments staged and filmed by social psychologists.

Chapter 2 examines the evolution of Milgram's "Obedience to Authority" experiments as drama. Milgram ran many versions of his experiment, with widely varied results, but chose to film only one: version 25, which emphasized compliance. Staged over one weekend in May 1962, *Obedience* was filmed using concealed cameras and edited as a scientific report. I scrutinize outtakes, previously unexamined subject records, and Milgram's editing notes from a filmmaker's perspective. Thus, I aim to shed light on how Milgram's film was constructed as a narrative of obedience despite considerable evidence to the contrary.

Many of Milgram's participants saw the experiment as a test of character. Chapter 3 widens the lens to interrogate the stories told by Stanley Milgram's participants in group debriefs conducted by psychiatrist Dr. Paul Errera at the conclusion of the "Obedience to Authority" experiments. How did they make sense of their experiences? According to narrative sociologist Arthur Frank, "Whilst people tell their own individual stories they do so by adapting and combining the narrative types that cultures make available."[9] Scrutinizing subject records and interview transcripts, I explore the key narrative resources—in this case, primarily sourced from film and television—on which these participants drew.

The brutal 1964 murder of Kitty Genovese in New York became an American legend. The *New York Times* reported that thirty-eight witnesses saw the violent crime occur yet did nothing. An outpouring of anger and concern soon followed. When psychologist John Darley and his colleagues published their first experiments on the "Bystander Effect," they claimed that the more people witness an event, the less likely we will intervene. Another line of investigation, by Irving and Jane Piliavin, found there to be more Good Samaritans among us than is usually recognized. However, their work failed to capture the public imagination. Chapter 4 explores the cinematic stories and images that fixed a particular version of the Kitty Genovese murder in cultural memory, from the Good Samaritan parable to "true crime" narratives.

Chapter 5 examines Phillip Zimbardo's "Stanford Prison Experiment," the best-known psychology experiment of our era. In a prison simulation, Zimbardo assigned male student volunteers to the roles of guards or prisoners. Zimbardo's nonprofessional actors inhabited their characters 24/7 for twelve days. The chapter investigates the "Stanford Prison Experiment" as a drama of confinement and explores its evolution as drama in the context of influential independent theater and film productions of the 1960s and 1970s that were set in prisons. Thus, it builds on economist and documentary filmmaker Thibault Le Texier's forensic interrogation of Zimbardo's audiovisual archive.[10]

Chapter 6 traces key images through Phillip Zimbardo's early field tests and experiments. Via examining the visual motifs of broken windows and hooded people, I argue that the success of the "Standard Prison Experiment" was partly due to Zimbardo's talent for working the telling metaphor. More broadly, the chapter explores the strategies employed by social psychology to link its experimental dramas to real-world crimes.

If social psychology fell in love with the movies, can it be said that film and television reciprocated? Chapter 7 explores retellings of these experiments in film, television, and gallery contexts, from the *BBC Prison Experiment* (2001) reality television series, Rod Dickinson's *Milgram Re-enactment* (2004), and Alex Gibney's documentary *The Human Behaviour Experiments* (2006) to independent feature *The Experimenter* (2015). I also reflect on my own films, challenging Milgram's "Obedience to Authority"—the feature documentary *Shock Room* and the verbatim documentary *Experiment 20* (2018). How can filmmakers open new spaces for critical inquiry?

Stanford Prison Experiment (2015) was in development for more than thirty years, with Zimbardo in a consulting role. The version that finally reached the big screen was based on audiovisual recordings of the original experiment and Zimbardo's book *The Lucifer Effect: How Good People Turn Evil*. The penultimate chapter closely scrutinizes a draft of the screenplay for the independent feature *Stanford Prison Experiment* written by Tim Talbot with brief comments by Phillip Zimbardo. Building on research from screenplay studies, narrative psychology, and criminology, chapter 8 examines Zimbardo's telling and retelling of his life story as a redemption narrative—one that, over time, became more closely aligned to the American version popularized by Hollywood.

Chapter 9 draws on insights from legal studies, sociology, and social psychology to investigate how narrative patterns borrowed from film and television influence how we compose stories. The immersive theater production *The Justice Syndicate*, the result of a collaboration across theater and psychology, provides one key case study. How do you tell new stories when the old stories are broken?

I consider that the social psychology films I discuss are at least as important as the experiments they purport to document. I believe that bringing a filmmaker's eye and understanding to the processes of their making offers insights to both psychologists and film scholars.

The subtitle of this book is *How Social Psychology Fell in Love with the Movies*, which could just as easily have read: "How a Filmmaker Fell in Love with Social Psychology." I hope the book captures my fascination with a cluster of inventive experiments and films that tackle how we collectively behave under pressure.

CHAPTER 1

Setting the Scene

From the beginning, film and psychology seemed made for each other. The latter emerged as a distinct discipline at approximately the same time as the emergence of cinema in the late nineteenth century. Research laboratories were already equipped with devices designed to shed light on seeing and perception; it was not long before the motion picture camera was incorporated into experimental laboratories as a scientific instrument. However, for all the two fields had in common, there also existed key differences. Psychology was preoccupied with facts and data, whereas film leaned toward stories and emotions.

Film and visual culture have a vast and complex history. Film did not progress in a straight line from simpler to more complex forms; rather, it emerged in a series of projects and experiments that often overlapped with or circled back on each other. Cinema emerged in the late nineteenth century within a broader visual culture that drew on practices from the diverse fields of art, science, education, image production, and more. According to film historian Scott Curtis and coauthors, "This rich visual culture produced a complicated overlapping network of image-making traditions, innovations, borrowings and paintings, *tableaux vivants*, photography and other pictorial and projection practices."[1] We can also add theater to this list.

Likewise, there is no single point we can identify as the beginning of the documentary. However, many film historians have highlighted "the projection of slides for nonfiction purposes."[2] This includes projections accompanied by live performance, shadow play devoted to topical themes, and illustrated lectures.[3] One possible beginning is the magic lantern shows of seventeenth-century Europe. In the United States, film historian and documentary filmmaker Charles Musser has made a case for the public lectures of religious leaders of the American Enlightenment from the 1730s onward. Religious groups presented lectures drawing on a wide range of illustrative materials: "models, charts, demonstrations, paintings, panoramas, reenactments, quotations from literary or musical sources, and even very occasional lantern slides."[4] I think there is also a case for twelfth-century Egyptian shadow playwright Ibn Daniyal, who drew his story lines from the streets around him.[5] Wherever we begin, performance was a central element in nonfiction screen practices and, later, documentary film.[6]

Science also has a long history of combining investigation and entertainment. In nineteenth-century Paris, neurologist Jean-Martin Charcot ran theatrical-style clinical demonstrations on a floodlit stage. He acted out the physical symptoms under discussion, including movements, gestures, and speech patterns. Charcot, who commissioned portraits of "hysterics" in hospitals, credited the still camera and its magnesium flash for some of his discoveries.[7] As Kate Flint wrote in her history of the flash, a sudden burst of brightness in the dark is often illuminating. If we fast-forward to the early twentieth century, psychologists in the United States performed theatrical-style presentations for introductory lectures, complete with demonstrations of laboratory equipment. Like Charcot, some professors were said to rehearse every word and move.[8] All part of building an audience for psychology.

Micro-motion Cinema

In the early twentieth century, Lillian and Frank Gilbreth, partners in life and work, were some of the first psychologists in on the motion picture game. Lillian held a doctorate in psychology, and Frank had a background as a scientific manager. Building on the work of Frederick Winslow Taylor, the American efficiency expert, the Gilbreths set out to study workers' movements: How could tasks best be broken down on the production line? What could they learn from the most efficient workers?

The Gilbreths began their studies with still photography and stereoscopic images—the latter to add depth to their images. Beginning in 1912, they incorporated the use of cinema into their studies of motion in the workplace. Hauling their bulky cameras and equipment onto factory floors, the Gilbreths created purpose-built laboratories on site (figure 1.1).[9] The pop-up experiment room could easily have been mistaken for an artist's studio. The floors and walls were whitewashed, and light poured in. Individual pieces of machinery were brought to the studio, and workers were asked to perform their usual tasks (figure 1.2). The psychologists photographed them and considered how workers could perform their movements in ways that were simpler, safer, and above all faster. Time was money. The Gilbreths called the resulting works "micro-motion cinema."

Once the film was developed, the couple returned to project the images to featured workers. Like the Lumière brothers and others before them, the Gilbreths found that people enjoyed seeing themselves photographed in the new medium of moving pictures.[10] Soon, returning to factories to screen films to participants

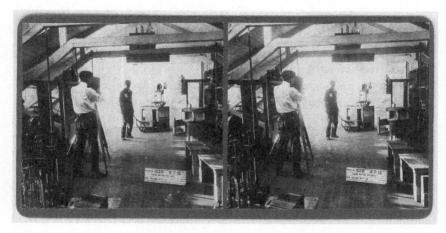

Figure 1.1. Stereoscope, filming in the Gilbreth experiment room, circa 1912. Courtesy of Cummings Center for History of Psychology, University of Akron.

Figure 1.2. Typing in the Gilbreth laboratory. Courtesy of Purdue University Libraries, Karnes Archives and Special Collections.

became a regular part of the Gilbreths' routine. The boundaries between art and science became blurred. A series of stereoscopes produced by the Gilbreths involved attaching small lights to workers' hands and bodies and filming them in motion (figure 1.3). The camera shutter was wide open to register every movement. The technique resulted in spellbinding images depicting light trails against

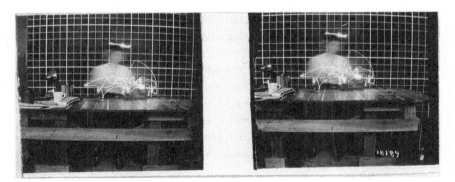

Figure 1.3. Cyclegraph in the Gilbreth laboratory, circa 1913. Courtesy of Purdue University Libraries, Karnes Archives and Special Collections.

ghostly backgrounds—now regarded as some of photography's earliest light paintings. Consequently, the Gilbreths' laboratory has been re-created for gallery installations, and their performances re-enacted.

The couple's documentaries are routinely credited to Frank Gilbreth. After all, he is the person often pictured behind the camera. However, the evidence suggests that Lillian Gilbreth played just as much of a role in the conception, planning, and realization of these films as her husband. Should she not be credited equally?

While the Gilbreths performed their micro-motion cinema experiments on the factory floor, Edwin Boring incorporated a hand-cranked projector into a makeshift psychology laboratory.[11] In 1916, Boring published a study on cinema and memory.[12] Central to his study is a sequence from Thomas Edison's short drama *Van Bieber's Experiment*. Walking home one night, an upper-class gentleman witnesses a burglar (who has been released recently from prison) in the act of stealing. Instead of reporting him, the gentleman forces the burglar to return the stolen goods, takes him home, and gives him a new set of clothes. The burglar is soon confronted with a reflection of his better self in a mirror and, thus, set on the path to reform. Mirrors, reflections, and doubles all featured extensively in early cinema. In some places, cinema itself was even thought of as a living mirror.[13] Yet, peering at one's reflection rarely led to anything good; one was often confronted with the darker side of one's nature. However, *Van Bieber's Experiment* was one of the United States' favorite narratives—a redemption story.

"I am going to show you a picture upon the wall," instructed Edward Boring to the participants in his psychology experiment. "I want you to watch it with your best attention."[14] After the screening, the subjects were asked to report everything they recalled and answer a written questionnaire. Thus, Boring demonstrated how a film fragment could be repurposed in a psychology laboratory to shed light on eyewitness accounts and individual memory. His experiment highlighted one aspect of moving pictures that gradually achieved increasing significance. Cinema was given a starring role as a metaphor for the processes of individual and social memory—films were memories that never faded.

Working on this project, I recalled my father's tips on making inquiries. I watched early movies about detectives and read investigators' manuals. One of the first detective manuals arrived on the scene in 1916. In his practical training manual, Emerson Manning described the art of shadowing as keeping a person, building, or premises under surveillance. Manning emphasized the importance of effective notetaking; valuable information should never be trusted to memory.[15]

SHOWMEN

"The screen provided a more universal textbook than laboratories could ever become," announced Hugo Münsterberg in 1916.[16] The Harvard professor of psychology was speaking at the Paramount Pictures launch of its new pictograph series. A magazine on screen, the series would help the United States and its citizens as they prepared to enter World War I. The term *pictograph* literally meant "picture writing," and the series would comprise short nonfiction programs in the form of animations. Proposed contributors ranged from former president Theodore Roosevelt to military experts, war correspondents, artists, and even magicians. While newsreels were records of events, Münsterberg claimed that pictographs would be "simulators of thought; socially, politically, educationally, morally, ethically."[17] Münsterberg's own contribution, *Testing the Mind*, would teach audiences how to become psychologists. Specifically, they would learn how to conduct tests for the relatively new field of vocational guidance. *Testing the Mind* would encourage self-reflection and democratize psychology.

This represents another possible beginning of the relationship between film and psychology. Before accepting a position at Harvard in 1892, Münsterberg trained at the University of Leipzig. After establishing his own laboratory, he conducted research on perception. Subsequently, William James recruited Münsterberg to run Harvard's first experimental psychology laboratory. Over the next two decades, Münsterberg produced textbooks, scientific articles, and think pieces for the popular press at an astonishing rate. Along the way, he contributed to a wide range of subfields, including forensic, industrial, and business psychology. He also moonlighted as a film theorist; *The Photo-Play* was one of the first books to examine the possibilities of cinema.[18]

Münsterberg himself attracted a great deal of press attention. In 1907, he set out to interrogate Harry Orchard, a self-confessed murder in a high-profile case. Having been commissioned by a popular magazine to do so, Münsterberg visited Orchard in his prison cell and undertook a series of psychological tests with a device he called the "chronoscope."[19] The introduction of scientific instruments involved its own brand of drama. "River, water, hill, pipe": the two men participated in a call-and-response activity as observers crowded around them. Münsterberg measured both Orchard's responses and his degree of hesitation. There was even a sequence that allegedly confirmed Orchard's guilt.

Claiming the chronoscope as one of the most remarkable scientific instruments ever produced, Münsterberg provided expert opinions to the court based on his tests. He claimed that the deliberations of judges, juries, attorneys, and detectives would no longer be required: a "microscope of the mind, it (the chronoscope could read a person's innermost thoughts and provide definitive evidence on their innocence or guilt."[20] He also claimed that future iterations of such psychological instruments would be able to detect truth and lies with absolute certainty. Münsterberg's account of his administration of the truth-telling test was reported widely. Many more such stunts followed.

Among the many criticisms directed at Münsterberg were that his experimental results were frequently written up in the popular press rather than scholarly outlets. (The same criticism was made of Philip Zimbardo many decades later.) Legal authority Charles Moore publicly dismissed Münsterberg's work as "yellow psychology." Thus, he compared applied psychology to "yellow journalism," which refers to sensationalist reporting, such as "crime news, scandal, and gossip, divorces and sex, and . . . the reporting of disasters and sports."[21] Such news relied on fake interviews and stories, making "lavish use of pictures" and inviting abuses such as "faked pictures" and "picture-stealing." Images, it seemed, were particularly suspect.

In public, Münsterberg promoted Paramount's new series and his own contribution. Behind the scenes, however, production did not proceed smoothly. His role was confined predominantly to writing the scenarios and reviewing work in progress. After viewing rough cuts of some of the films in 1915, the psychologist demanded the studio call a halt to production. Jumbled letters that formed part of a psychological test were introduced by a range of animated characters. He claimed that this lack of standardization would distract audiences and threaten the validity of his on-screen experiments,[22] and live-action sequences should replace the animation. After a change of management in 1916, Paramount discontinued *Testing the Mind*.

While Münsterberg courted Hollywood, Sigmund Freud declined its calls. Sam Goldwyn was just one of several movie moguls who hoped Freud might sign on as a scenario writer. Before he departed for Europe in 1924, Goldwyn announced that he planned to offer Dr. Freud US$100,000 to write a love story for the screen.[23] When asked what talent he expected to bring back, Goldwyn said: "I'm going over to get this man Freud. We need somebody to throw a lot of good old sizzling heart stuff into pictures. They tell me this Freud knows how to dish it."[24] However, Freud's terse reply was that he did not intend to see Goldwyn. The founder of psychoanalysis also rejected colleague Karl Abraham's proposal to make an educational documentary based on a clinical case to be supervised

Figure 1.4. Arnold Gesell working in his photographic dome, Yale University, 1947.
Herbert Gehr/The LIFE Picture Collection/Shutterstock.

by a senior analyst. Now, it seems ironic that "the talking cure" was to be investigated via silent film. Freud feared that the medium could not do justice to
abstract ideas. "Stupid things happen in film affairs," Freud later wrote, object-
ing to a German studio's plans to film a script entitled *Secrets of a Soul*, allegedly
based on the psychoanalyst's confidential notebooks.[25] Initially, at least, it was
experimental psychologists, rather than their psychoanalytical colleagues, who
were more attracted to the movies.

Methods of Observation

In the United States and Europe in the 1920s, psychologists who used observa-
tional methodologies to learn more about child development swapped film for
the detailed diaries, sketches, and still photographs on which they had previously relied. Movie cameras soon began to be featured as developmental psychologists filmed real-life behavior and interactions.

A photograph shows a man in a white laboratory coat interacting with a baby
in a cot. Placed in the center of a glass dome, the two are brightly lit (figure 1.4).
In the shadows surrounding the dome women observe. Perhaps one of them is

Figure 1.5. Kurt Lewin filming in project room, 1939. Courtesy of Frederick Kent Collection, Special Collections and Archives, University of Iowa Libraries.

the mother of the baby participating in the research?[26] From the 1920s onward, psychologist Arnold Gesell regularly used film and photography in his studies of child development at Yale. A purpose-built photographic dome was surrounded by a one-way vision screen to conceal observers. Gesell claimed that the film camera records behavior "in such coherent, authentic and measurable detail that . . . the reaction patterns of infant and child become almost as tangible as tissue."[27] Like many of his colleagues, Gesell valued motion pictures as a means of shedding light on processes, and the film camera was claimed as an instrument for the psychology laboratory.

I am looking at a black-and-white photograph taken in 1939 (figure 1.5). Two men in suits stand on a table in a room that is bright at one end and dark at the other. This production still from a documentary shot by Kurt Lewin depicts Lewin's "project room" at the University of Iowa. One man's body blocks a camera on a tripod as he peers into the lens—he is the cinematographer. Lewin leans toward him. A handful of observers are seated behind the experimenters; all eyes are on a small group of children playing together. Practical lights—the filmmaking term for everyday lights placed within the set—are trained on the children. A clock is prominent. As viewers, we are positioned as observers. Our gaze is directed toward the children in the lit area as if they were on a stage.[28]

Kurt Lewin is regarded as one of the founders of social psychology, a field that studies social behavior via experiments. He was introduced to moving pictures through home movies. A film enthusiast, Lewin initially bought his own camera and film. Later, he had access to a 35 mm camera (owned by the Psychological Institute of Berlin) capable of filming longer sequences; he soon incorporated film in his child observation studies. Researchers typically filmed children at play through a small opening in a tent.[29] In a lecture, Lewin explained that "an implicit reason for using film is to document the effect of ecological conditions and social milieu in the development of children."[30] At this time, movies made by psychologists were often referred to as film demonstrations. They were accompaniments to lectures rather than the starring attraction.

In the late 1930s, Lewin and graduate student Ronald Lippitt conducted an influential series of experiments at the Iowa Child Welfare Research Station. Small groups of children were exposed to different styles of leadership and social climates described as "democratic," "authoritarian," and "laissez-faire." The experiments were inspired by Lewin's own flight from Germany during the rise of fascism in the 1930s. In a departure from his previous studies, in these experiments graduate students stepped into the laboratory and acted out the different leadership styles.[31] A makeshift laboratory was created in the attic of a university building—a space more often associated with horror movies than social drama. The project room doubled as a clubhouse for participants and an observation space for the experimenters. Small groups of boys met once a week and participated in activities such as making theatrical masks. Four graduate students acted as "leaders," switching groups every six weeks. The researchers took great care to create consistency in the behaviors associated with the different leadership styles. Observers generated lists of actions and statements classified as democratic, autocratic or laissez-faire. The "leaders" continuously observed each other and provided feedback on techniques.[32] Javier Lezaun has identified this as a key moment in the history of psychology: the beginning of a tradition in the social sciences in which "the experimenter strives to exploit, rather than minimize, the potential of his interactions."[33]

Film records were critical in understanding the group dynamics under investigation. The resulting documentary, *Experimental Studies in the Social Climates of Groups*, was described by its distributors as "a classic study by Kurt Lewin in which a hidden camera observes three boys' clubs operated under autocratic, democratic, and *laissez-faire* principles. Shows how boys react when conditions of leadership are changed to another method." A narration track and graphics were added to selected black-and-white actuality footage. The narrator—presumably one of the experimenters—provides some background and outlines the researchers' key conclusions. The autocratic climate, for example, was observed to kill individual initiative, while the democratic climate resulted in higher levels of cooperation and a free exchange of ideas. Significantly, Lewin did not claim the footage as evidence. The film's narrator explicitly states that "these unrehearsed motion pictures document the activities of the club. They are offered as illustration not as scientific proof."[34]

World War II was a watershed moment in the history of psychology. Large numbers of clinical psychologists, psychiatrists, and associated experts were drafted to screen recruits, assess morale, and treat the casualties of war.[35] Training and educational documentaries featuring psychologists also played their part. According to film scholar Noah Tsika, both during and after the war, the U.S. military "sought to formalize and expand the links between cinema and social sciences."[36] For example, the Psychological Test Film Unit of the Army Air Forces First Motion Picture Unit studied the effects of cinema on audiences. Short "tests on film" were screened as diagnostic tools, and films were also used to treat war trauma. The latter practice had precedents in World War I, when British and French doctors screened Charlie Chaplin's films in an attempt to restore speech to shellshocked soldiers. Cinema was particularly valued due to its capacity to trigger emotion. In *Introduction to Combat Fatigue* (1944), a typical documentary of the time, a U.S. Navy psychiatrist addressed traumatized servicemen and provided counseling. The film's dramatic re-enactments aimed to desensitize service personnel to the sights and sounds of battle. Fear was a fighting man's friend, according to the documentary's narrator. Viewers should expect to feel uncomfortable, advised the psychiatrist-narrator: "When we dislodge sore feelings, we have to pry a little—like a sore tooth. And that hurts."[37] Re-enactments often featured both professional and nonprofessional actors. It was hoped that traumatized military personnel might manage their dark impulses by "acting them out."[38] However, military psychology films were aimed primarily at treating individuals suffering from combat trauma rather than as a means of staging experiments into social dynamics.

HIDDEN CAMERAS

Allen Funt, the creator of the television series *Candid Camera*, credited the inspiration for his long-running hit to his experiences during the war. Psychologists praised *Candid Camera* as "a repository of extremely valuable observations of human behavior" that offered some advantages over laboratory experiments.[39] Recordings were made without subjects' knowledge; therefore, there was no chance their responses would be influenced by the biases of the experimenter.

The hidden camera technique also eliminated the possibility that the laboratory setting itself could influence people's behavior. Moreover, *Candid Camera* combined entertainment and research. How did one of the world's first factual television programs come to be assigned such a starring role in psychology and the social sciences? Do those claims stand up to scrutiny?

In his memoir, Allen Funt wrote about the show's origins.[40] The program was inspired by his background as a social science student. As a research assistant at Cornell University, Funt worked with Kurt Lewin on experiments on the behavior of women and children. After completing his undergraduate degree, Funt was accepted into an executive training group at a New York department store. As it turned out, there was no executive training on offer—this store was simply recruiting extra people power for the Christmas rush. Funt's next job was in the art department of an advertising agency. This led to an invitation to develop "gags and gimmicks" for radio shows. When World War II broke out, Funt was drafted into the U.S. Army, where he recorded soldiers' letters home and created radio shows to boost morale. Until then, the only audio recording equipment Funt could access was bulky. However, thanks to technology captured from the Germans, Funt found himself in possession of "the smallest, most advanced portable recorder of that era."[41] Thus, skits and gags involving hidden microphones became a real possibility. In the late 1940s, these assignments led to the radio program *Candid Microphone*.[42] One journalist wrote that *Candid Microphone* was "a show in which anyone could tune in on their neighbors."[43] However, not everyone saw this as a good thing; some audience members felt that the early programs were cruel to the victims of the hoaxes.

Based on the radio program, the American Broadcasting Corporation signed *Candid Camera* the following year. The program took the camera out into the city; it was often hidden behind a folding screen with the cameraperson shooting through a two-way mirror.[44] Each skit was brief and self-contained. The humor of the situation could be understood quickly by audiences. Funt described the program as catching a person "in the act of being himself."[45]

I watch an episode from the first series broadcast on television. The camera pans over a group of framed photographs of people in the city. The off-screen presenter announces, "This is the *Candid Camera* program which brings you secretly made movies of all kinds of people." Funt tells the audience that the best way to understand the *Candid Camera* concept is to watch a segment. In a sketch filmed in a department store with a hidden camera, a series of women return items of clothing and seek refunds. To their surprise and bafflement, the salesman refuses to exchange or issue refunds for faulty goods. Eventually, the salesman—a stooge employed by the show's producers—lets his customers in on the joke. "Let me tell you something," he tells one woman. "Have you ever been in a movie? Would you like to see yourself on television?" Recognizing that she has been hoaxed, the woman collapses in laughter.[46]

Figure 1.6. *Candid Camera*, Allen Funt, 1964.

Watching *Candid Camera*, I was initially struck by some similarities to late-night shows that combine comedy sketches with social commentary. However, the similarities did not go much further than opening titles featuring city sky-lines and a genial host. The program's slapstick-style formula relied on captur-ing the embarrassment of people caught on camera. As a comedy style, slapstick often involves exaggerated physical activity in everyday life that can lead to mis-haps. *Candid Camera*'s hoaxes included talking and moving mailboxes or devices on lunch counters that advised diners not to eat until a light flashed—the light, of course, never flashed (figure 1.6). Audiences were able to observe people's bafflement and consternation. On *Candid Camera*, amateurs provided the physical comedy usually performed by professional entertainers.

The aired segments of *Candid Camera* were the result of extended planning and preparation. Funt estimated that only three or four incidents of every fifty filmed were broadcast.[47] I imagine those outtakes would have made interesting viewing. People caught on camera did not always perform to order, and not every joke succeeded. The behavior that audiences witnessed was hardly typical. Film historian Fred Nadis has taken issue with Funt's claim that the program simply exposed human frailties. In his view, *Candid Camera*'s formula involved "expos-ing an individual's vanity, greed or weakness in the face of social pressure."[48] *Candid Camera* placed people under social pressure as entertainment (figure 1.7).

Figure 1.7. *Candid Camera*, Allen Funt, 1965.

The films of social psychologists shared this interest while also changing the genre to explore the darker side of human behavior.

GOING UNDERCOVER

In American newspapers of the 1950s, stories of the House Committee on Un-American Activities, "Reds," and brainwashing appear alongside reports of new findings regarding the psychology of small groups and techniques of persuasion. Discussion of psychology studies was confined to the Sunday papers, alongside book reviews and opinion columns. They aimed to provide readers with new insights into human behavior. Social psychology was having a moment. It was said that the small group interactions in which psychologists such as Solomon Asch and Leon Festinger specialized could be applied to the dynamics most people encountered in offices, schools, and even families.

The most influential social psychology experiments left a trail of visual evidence. Others simply read like film scripts and, in some cases, embraced the tragicomic. Leon Festinger and his collaborators went so far as to infiltrate a social movement to study it, although calling the Seekers a social movement might be stretching the truth a little. In late September 1954, a story appeared in the *Lake City Herald* with the headline "Prophecy from Another Planet. Clarion

Call to City: Flee That Flood. It'll Swamp Us on December 21, Outer Space Tells Suburbanite." Readers were told that creatures from a planet called Clarion had contacted a suburban housewife, advising her that a flood would swamp the city on December 21. Mrs. Marion Keen of 847 West School Street, Lake City, Florida, said that the visitors from outer space, whom she described as superior beings, had observed fault lines in the earth's crust from their flying saucers. The west coast of the Americas, from Seattle to Chile, would be submerged. The researchers seized the opportunity to study a potential social movement in the making. They contacted Mrs. Keene. "Prophecy from Another Planet" would provide an opportunity to run a "field test" of their ideas about dissonance. Festinger and his colleagues soon hired observers to gather information about the conviction and commitment of people who joined the fledgling movement.

The group of psychologists, sociologists, and their students posed as ordinary members of the group—that is, they went undercover. According to Festinger, their study could not have been conducted otherwise. The researchers used a range of methods to introduce themselves. Initially, one of the investigators simply called Mrs. Keene and asked to talk about those matters she had discussed with a journalist; he then followed up with a visit. Another two researchers traveled to Lake City two weeks later. One called Mrs. Keene, introducing himself as a businessman who traveled a lot and had an interest in flying saucers. He later brought back one of his coauthors, who was introduced as a business associate. Next, a sociology student was recruited as an observer so the team had someone on the ground; he was given a cover story about his psychic experiences. A young woman was trained as an observer and was provided with a cover story about a troubling dream to render her interest credible. The latter two observers were particularly welcomed since they appeared to be in tune with the universe.

I found myself watching *Sherlock Jr.*, Buster Keaton's 1924 film that depicts a movie projectionist using a manual to teach himself how to be a detective.[49] Professional training for investigators was still in its infancy. In one scene, Sherlock Jr. attempts to put the textbook's rule 5 into practice: "Shadow your man closely." Taking the advice rather too literally, the would-be crime buster keeps step with his suspect, mirroring his every action in broad daylight. Sherlock Jr. is soon caught out and becomes the pursued rather than the pursuer. Executed with split-second comic timing, the physical action involves a hair-raising chase along the tops of train carriages and hanging from a water tower. As with so much of Keaton's comedy, however, there is more to this than meets the eye. *Sherlock Jr.* explores the fuzzy lines between the observer and the observed.

Festinger and his colleagues wanted to understand how members of groups that espoused particular ideologies took actions that were consistent with their beliefs, in addition to the extent to which they tried to convince others. The researchers acknowledged they had been too successful—their intervention reinforced the group's beliefs. There appeared to have been an upsurge in membership, with four mysterious new members joining the group in ten days. All were outsiders with no obvious links to the local community. Thus, Mrs. Keene and her followers believed that someone was looking out for them. Mrs. Keene channeled information from a man calling himself Captain Video, which was also the name of a popular television show of the time. His message? A flying saucer would land in her backyard at midnight on a specified day to pick up the chosen ones. The Seekers began preparations in earnest. What actually happened on the appointed day?[50] I will return to this story in chapter 9.

Reading about these experiments now, it is hard not to think of two groups—the Seekers and the observers. One group went undercover, infiltrating a fledgling group and conducting intensive surveillance. Perhaps this is another reason I identify with social psychologists? Both gravitate toward observer roles. Filmmakers are the people always watching events from the shadows, behind the camera. According to director Anne Bogart, film and theater practitioners are essentially "orchestrators of social interaction."[51]

Salesmen

In 1964, psychologists gathered at Cornell University to evaluate *Candid Camera* as a tool for research and teaching purposes. Participants included academics from psychology, sociology, and education departments; publishing houses; research agencies; and, perhaps most important, representatives of the American Psychology Association, which sponsored the seminar. A core group of roughly twenty people was present for the entire four days, and many others drifted in and out of the meeting. Beforehand, Richard Evans had outlined an agenda based on viewing *Candid Camera* segments in categories related to key psychology topics, including conformity, cognitive dissonance, extreme incidents involving tolerance and intolerance, and child behavior. The timetable was organized such that a segment would be aired, followed by a discussion about its relevance to research or teaching.[52]

It probably will not surprise anyone familiar with the social dynamics of academia to learn that, by the end of the first day, the group was split. Only a small number of participants were interested in research, while the majority wished to explore how *Candid Camera* could be used in classrooms. The latter group prevailed, and the remaining days would also focus on teaching applications. The initial categories proposed were suggested by Funt. At the end of the symposium, it was agreed that a more comprehensive categorization of the *Candid Camera* materials was required. The production company would make a financial contribution to any university department interested in taking on the task. (The archive of programs ended up at Stanford University.) Following the proceedings, Funt was given a plaque to memorialize his contributions to understanding human behavior.[53] His enthusiastic interest in the academic community was much appreciated. No doubt, it also assisted sales. After all, the *Candid Camera* showrunner initiated the gathering. Funt was building a franchise.

Opinions about *Candid Camera* and its creator were sharply divided; filmmakers and psychologists did not see eye to eye on the matter. "Allen Funt is known variously as the folksy creator of *Candid Camera*, as a successful aggressive television producer and a difficult man with a considerable sense of his own worth"—this is how Harrison Engle introduced his interview with Funt for *Film Comment* the following year.[54] It is an illuminating exchange; while simultaneously courteous and well-informed, Engle signaled that there would be no holds barred. In his view, the producer belonged to the tradition of the huckster or circus barker. Funt was "plainly commercial, operating with a minimum of aesthetic, moral and philosophical considerations."[55] In part, the story of the symbiotic relationship that developed between social psychology and film and television involves showpeople and stunts. Hidden cameras were treated as truth-telling machines resembling Münsterberg's chronoscope.

The postwar decades represented a golden age of social psychology. The best-known experiments utilized hidden cameras to reveal aspects of human behavior. The classic experiments were conducted in purpose-built settings—like Milgram's psychology laboratory or Zimbardo's prison—or public locations. The latter included institutions, streets, and buses or trains. Whatever the setting, however, experimenters now consciously linked their studies to real-world events: the Holocaust, the rape and murder of Kitty Genovese, the Attica Prison riot.

We arrive now at another possible beginning—Stanley Milgram. From the outset, he was up-front about his debt to the arts: "Although experiments in chemistry and physics often involve shiny equipment, flasks and electronic gear, an experiment in social psychology smacks much more of dramaturgy and theatre."[56] I had Milgram and his film *Obedience* in my sights.

CHAPTER 2

"You're an Actor Now"

It was October 1961. A man later given the pseudonym "Fred Prozi," approximately fifty years old and unemployed, made his way toward the Yale University campus. By late afternoon, the temperature had dropped to 14°C (57.2°F). Wearing a jacket and no tie, Prozi made his way down Chapel Street and turned left onto High Street. He walked under the clock archway and arrived at Linsly-Chittenden Hall. Gazing up at the facade of the imposing building, he lit a cigarette. The US$4.50 he would earn from participating in a psychology experiment would cover a beer or two later. These are some of the facts known about Fred Prozi, featured as the obedient character in Stanley Milgram's book *Obedience to Authority* (1974). But are they facts?

FACTS

Scientists trawl through data, looking for patterns, analyzing, and testing. In the process, traces of the individual, the idiosyncratic, are often stripped from the story. As a filmmaker, it is my task to put all this back in—to seek the stories that can be recovered from the margins of the experimenter's notebook, edge numbers on a strip of celluloid, footage that did not make the final cut, the experimenter's scrawl on a subject record, or the idle conversations at the beginning of an audio recording of an experimental session. These are also clues. As historian Arlette Farge wrote, "An archival document is a tear in the fabric of time . . . an unplanned glimpse offered into an unexpected event."[1]

We are now watching black-and-white film footage. A man in a white polo shirt sits at a shock machine (figure 2.1). He gazes at the lever that will inflict potentially lethal electric shocks on his victim. "Please continue," says the Experimenter. The man protests, but at the next prompt, he pushes the lever. He pushes it over and over again. However, he never stops protesting.

Figure 2.1. *Obedience*, Stanley Milgram, 1965.

This is a scene from *Obedience* (1965), one of the most influential documentaries of the postwar era, screened continuously over more than five decades since its production, in lecture hall presentations, in broadcasts, and as clips in other documentaries. Its dramatic scenario has also inspired numerous feature films, reality television programs, and re-enactments. As Jerome Bruner argued, humans make sense of experiences primarily through stories, and the dramatization of events enables them to be integrated more easily into the social order.[2] Therefore, stories offer some advantages over facts. Stanley Milgram claimed his documentary to be the objective record of a scientific experiment. Yet, his "Obedience to Authority" experiments provided as much evidence of people's refusal to follow harmful orders as they did their willingness to obey them. Although he ran more than thirty variations of what he described as a "laboratory drama," Milgram chose to film only one. This is an important fact to keep in mind. The film was version 5, in which a clear majority of people obeyed orders. How did Milgram shape his data into one particular narrative from many potential scenarios? I am particularly interested in how documentary participants were selected on the strength of their performances and gradually shaped to become more like their fictional film counterparts.

Milgram's documentary captured my imagination as a young adult. I cannot recall precisely where I first saw it. Was it in Psychology 101 as an arts student?

Or as part of our boot camp–style training for a residential care position working with teenagers in trouble with the law? As it happened, I bailed out of both
that particular course and community work to pursue a career as a filmmaker.
Obedience was one of the films that set me on that path. I found its drama compelling but was uneasy about Milgram's conclusions. Were we really pro-
grammed to obey? I pursued postgraduate work in film and history. Many years
later, in 2008, I began ordering materials from Yale University's Sterling Memo-
rial Library, where Milgram's extensive archive of documents is held. The "permission to inspect" form described my topic as "Stanley Milgram as Filmmaker."
I remember the excitement of examining new pieces of the puzzle—from script
notes and film budgets to recordings and transcripts.

There were over one hundred boxes of materials in Milgram's archive at Yale.
I made my way through many of them, searching for images and voices from
the past. Historian Natalie Davis has written about her lifelong love affair with
archives. Working for a lengthy period in Lyon, poring over medieval records,
Davis realized she had formed a powerful memory association between her
research and the actual archives: "The room itself became closely identified with
the traces of the past I was examining; the smell of its old wood, the shape of its
windows, the sounds from the cobblestones or running stream." Davis also wrote
that "the room itself was a threshold on which I would meet papers that had been
handled and written on by the people of the past."[3]

While I was working with Milgram's materials, I watched Twentieth Century
Fox's *Call Northside 777* (1948), a feature film in the genre termed *semidocumentary noir*, a fictionalized account of the real-life reinvestigation of a crime
(figures 2.2 and 2.3). In 1932, Joseph Majczek was sentenced to life imprisonment
for killing a Chicago police officer. A decade later, his mother advertised for any
additional evidence—she maintained that her son was innocent. In the film,
James Stewart played a newspaper reporter, P. J. McNeal, assigned to the story
as a human interest piece. Initially skeptical, McNeal gradually became caught
up in the quest to overturn the verdict. His investigation hinged on the search
for a missing piece of visual evidence.

Doubt is central to the historical method. Facts are only as good as the documents they rest upon, said historian Lynn Hunt. In that regard, "the historian is
like a detective, lawyer or investigative journalist sifting through information,
analyzing and comparing sources, written or not, and using every possible forensic procedure to get at the truth, that is, the facts of the case."[4] The writing of
history, said Carlo Ginzburg, inevitably involves construction: "We put together
bits and pieces of what has come down to us through the ages to create a picture
of the past. However, that picture is itself a *reconstruction*."[5] As a filmmaker in
the archives, I aim to reintroduce doubt into discussions of *Obedience* as evidence. I want to refashion a closed text as an open text—the former points toward
a single point of view, while the latter is open to multiple interpretations.[6] The

Figure 2.2. *Call Northside 777*, Twentieth Century Fox, 1948.

Figure 2.3. *Call Northside 777*, Twentieth Century Fox, 1948.

obstacles encountered in the research process and its limitations are necessarily part of such an account. As Ginzburg proposed, "Hypotheses, doubts, the uncertainties become part of the narrative, the *search for truth* become part of the (necessarily incomplete) truth."[7]

LABORATORY DRAMA

Experimenters claimed laboratory simulations such as "Obedience to Authority" as data. Yet, from the very beginning, simulations combined both drama and data. According to Thomas Blass, the social psychology experiments of the 1960s owed as much to stagecraft as to science.[8] Stanley Milgram's dramaturgical skills could already be seen in the doctoral research he undertook in Norway and France. In an experiment inspired by those of his postgraduate adviser Solomon Asch, Milgram investigated national differences in conformity. He used props and prerecorded dialogue to create the sense that there was a group of subjects in the laboratory, although there was only one. The script for the *Obedience* experimental drama was more complex and progressed through multiple iterations on the way to staging. The experimental script that underpinned both the "Obedience to Authority" trials and the documentary *Obedience* was authored by Milgram and workshopped in his laboratory. A "structured improvisation," it combines scripted and improvised elements.

Milgram described the conception of his "Obedience to Authority" experiments in musical terms; they were "variations on a theme" on the work of Solomon Asch. Specifically, they built on Asch's "conformity and independence" experiments in which subjects were asked to guess the length of lines on paper amid a group of peers instructed to give the wrong answer. Milgram set out to raise the dramatic stakes and tackle a problem of great significance. There was another sense, though, in which Milgram's obedience dramas aspired to be variations on a theme. Per the *Harvard Dictionary of Music*, a set of variations allows for subtler, more graduated bridges between each piece than would be possible with simple, polar opposites. In each musical variation, some elements remain the same while others change. By the time we hear the closing theme, our understanding of the piece has been transformed. In much the same way, Milgram's film, version 25—a reprise of version 5—shifts our understanding of the whole series.

The obedience experiments began with a pilot study Milgram conducted with his students in late 1960. Keenly aware of the value of images, he took behind-the-scenes photographs of some sessions. Along with Milgram's comments, selected stills formed part of a successful funding application to the National Science Foundation for the complete experiments.[9] Shot on low-contrast black-and-white Kodak Plus X stock (rated at 120 ASA), these photographs have less dramatic impact than those taken during the full experimental trials. The subjects, clean-cut young men drawn from the Yale University student population, are dressed neatly in shirts and ties. The shock machine prototype, which features in several close-ups, is far more rudimentary than the more professional model Milgram later produced.[10] Over the following year, Milgram went to a great deal of trouble to script his laboratory drama, design its setting and key props, and cast men in the roles of Experimenter and Victim.

Between 1960 and 1962, Stanley Milgram invited more than 800 men (and some women) to his purpose-built laboratory, where he ran a set of precisely calibrated experiments on obedience and resistance to authority. Subjects were told they were participating in an experiment on learning and memory. In a carefully scripted scenario, they were assigned the role of Teacher in a three-way drama whose dramatis personae were as follows: the Experimenter supervised each experimental session, and the Learner (often called the Victim) posed as a volunteer subject and then took their place at the shock machine. In the best-known versions of Milgram's experiment (and the one that was filmed), the Victim was in another room. Heard but not seen, their prerecorded protests and screams were played each time the Victim was punished. The Teachers were volunteers from New Haven and the surrounding area who responded to an advertisement stating: "We will pay you $4.00 for one hour of your time. Persons needed for a Study of Memory."[11]

The cover story Milgram devised was that the volunteers were administering a learning and memory test to aid scientific researchers. Teachers were not aware that the other two roles (Experimenter and Victim) were played by Stanley Milgram's associates—"confederates," in the language of psychology of that era. The Victim responded to an advertisement seeking part-time assistants for a scientific experiment. Nonprofessional actors are often thought to add veracity to the roles they play. Director Henry Watts, a key figure in the British story-documentary movement of the 1930s and 1940s, claimed that the awkwardness nonprofessional actors brought to their movements and gestures in front of the camera provided an additional level of authenticity.[12]

Milgram's choice for the Experimenter role was the stern-looking John Williams, a local high school science teacher. By contrast, he described New Haven accountant James McDonough as "brilliant for the victim." Milgram observed that McDonough, who had worked as an accountant for the railways for twenty-five years and had eight children, was "mild and submissive, not at all academic." Milgram cast McDonough despite expressing reservations that he "could not act too well."[13] These men played assigned roles—rather than versions of themselves—within Milgram's drama. (The two teams that played the Experimenter and Victim in "Obedience to Authority" were nonprofessional actors who benefited from a scripted scenario, rehearsals, and a long-running show.) Their preparation was tightly supervised by Milgram, who described his confederates as "trained for their roles." Any good Experimenter used role play when setting up a laboratory simulation, doing a dry run with his assistants to see how the procedure flowed, Milgram said. He paid considerable attention to external aspects of performance, including costume, gesture, and the delivery of the scripted lines. In pretrials in the summer of 1961, Milgram went so far as to play the Victim role himself to demonstrate the kind of performance he wanted.[14]

Milgram described the essence of his drama thus: "A person comes into a laboratory and is asked to carry out a series of acts that increasingly come into conflict with their conscience."[15] The experimental script unfolded in three sequences: first, the Arrival and Cover Story; second, the Experimenter–Teacher–Learner Encounter; and, third, the Psychologist–Subject–Confederates Debrief. The first sequence was typed up as a ten-page script titled "Experimenter's Instructions and Procedure as Given to the Subject."[16] It most closely resembles a theater script, with written dialogue and brief descriptions of dramatic action. By the time he ran version 5, Milgram had revised the script so that the Victim mentioned a minor heart problem. The main part of the drama was partly improvised around his dramatic scenario and a series of key lines given to the Experimenter. As Milgram wrote, "An experiment in social psychology smacks of dramaturgy or theater. The experimenter carefully constructs a scenario to focus on certain aspects of behavior, a scenario in which the end is unknown and completed by the experimental subject."[17]

The first audiences for "Obedience to Authority" were the visitors Milgram invited to watch experimental sessions with him behind the two-way mirror in his laboratory. During the pilot studies, Milgram and his students watched the sessions unfold together. They were astonished by what they saw. Milgram later also invited colleagues, noting that "young Yale professors invited to view the experiments left exhilarated."[18] Milgram's research assistant, Alan Elms, recalled, "Behind the two-way mirrors, Stanley Milgram and I (as well as occasional visitors) watched each early subject with fascination and with our own share of tension."[19] The sessions soon lost the sense of an artificially constructed experiment. "Obedience to Authority" presented slice after slice of real life, with moral decisions made and unmade every evening. To that extent, it resembles the medieval morality play *Everyman*, in which a man is summoned by God's Messenger. Everyman must immediately provide a complete accounting of his life. A host of Virtues and Vices—dramatis personae based around single abstracted qualities such as Fellowship, Knowledge, Kindness, Beauty, and the Five Wits—could be called on to assist. Whereas fifteenth-century audiences watched the dramatic struggle for Everyman's soul, Milgram's colleagues watched participants struggle with their consciences. I imagine those neatly dressed young men being unsure how to respond, perhaps shuffling uncomfortably and checking their supervisor's expression as they tried not to make any noise and blow their cover.

It was October 1961. Fred Prozi made his way into the lobby of Linsly-Chittenden Hall.[20] It was after hours, and the building was deserted. Prozi took out a sheet of paper and scanned it. As instructed, he took the back stairs. In the darkness, every sound echoed—the gurgling of pipes, the slamming of a door, voices in the distance. In the basement, a young man in a lab coat appeared. "Mr. Prozi? Please step this way," he said. The rest is history—Fred Prozi did as he was told. These are the known facts. But are they really the facts?

DOCUMENTARY FILM

At the end of his experiments, Milgram set out to make a documentary film recording the events that had taken place in his laboratory. Otherwise, he feared, people simply would not believe him. Over the course of its production, the documentary and its story line evolved to highlight the most dramatic material rather than the full range of human behavior observed. In tracing the shaping of Milgram's *Obedience* documentary, I am not suggesting that editing film is an inherently manipulative act. All films and audiovisual narratives are edited, just as text is combined and rearranged to construct written narratives. However, I am suggesting that in the case of a film such as *Obedience*—routinely presented and understood as scientific evidence—we must review the footage and its construction as a documentary to consider the range of interpretations it may offer (figures 2.4 and 2.5). Milgram, who preserved much of his unreleased footage, argued that film provides researchers with richly textured records of human behavior that can be opened to further investigation.[21]

Milgram ran and filmed the experimental trials that featured in *Obedience* over one weekend in late May 1962. Fourteen men participated—thirteen of them in version 25, described as the "Film Condition," and one in the "Friend to Friend" version. (The latter aimed to test the degree to which people would be prepared to inflict shocks on a friend.) Other versions were staged for a brief sequence of stills. Subjects depicted in the film were unaware they were being filmed. According to the brief production notes Milgram later wrote for a press kit, their performances on arrival, at the shock machine, and during the debrief were spontaneous and unrehearsed.[22] Milgram noted, however, that the nonprofessional actor playing the Experimenter was nervous in front of the camera and talked more than usual.

In attempting to reconstruct the process of editing *Obedience*, I assembled the surviving materials. They included the preserved unreleased footage, an intriguing audiotape labeled "Instructions for Filmmaker," plus what I now believe to be Milgram's own editing notes, previously unexamined subject files, and production documentation. (To a filmmaker, budgets, invoices, and order forms all tell their own version of the production story.) While researchers had examined some of the materials related to the film, the subject records provided new insights.[23] I compared the preserved unreleased footage and the completed film and cross-referenced them with documentation. In the process, I worked with a film editor

Figure 2.4. *Obedience*, Stanley Milgram, 1965.

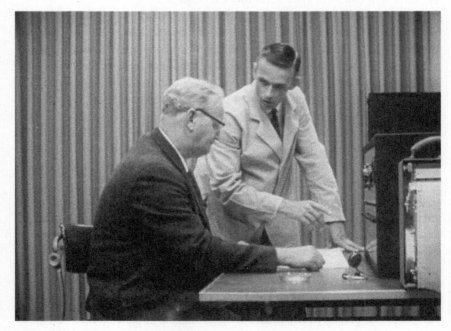

Figure 2.5. *Obedience*, Stanley Milgram, 1965.

to reconstruct the preserved *Obedience* footage. My aim was to clarify some of the decisions Milgram and his collaborators made as they authored the film.

Milgram's key collaborators for the shoot were Bill Stoneback and Ed English. The two men had some experience in producing educational films, and Stoneback was an employee at Yale's Audio/Visual Center. A week before the shoot, English provided a budget estimate, calculating that a 20-minute sound film could be produced for US$1,867. This budget provides a valuable overview of the filming methodology.[24] The documentary was to be shot on a 16 mm camera with 1,200-foot film magazines. Therefore, any individual take could run for approximately 30 minutes without interruption. Due to costs, Milgram ordered only enough film stock for a total of 180 minutes of shooting over three days. Consequently, the crew would need to frequently turn the camera on and off to save their limited supplies of film stock. Considerable effort was made to hide the filming apparatus from participants. Each day, it took two hours to set up the camera and hide the lights, sound recorder, and microphones. The budget estimate did not include any additional shooting or postproduction expenses. Milgram would need to raise additional funds to cover these costs later. Purchase orders for picture developing and work printing confirm the team shot the entire six rolls of film purchased. Approximately two-thirds of this footage has been preserved.

Editing notes are usually informal and contain the director's and editor's reactions to the footage; those for *Obedience* are no exception. Bill Stoneback constructed the assembly edit based on Milgram's evaluation of the material. It was previously thought that Chris Johnson, a graduate student who supervised the second phase of editing, made these notes.[25] On further examination, however, they appear to have been made by Milgram himself. Both the style of notes and the handwriting match those of Stanley Milgram, and Johnson has confirmed he did not make them (Chris Johnson, personal communication, 2012). One factor that may have been misleading is that Milgram wrote about himself in the third person.

It is revealing to review the editing notes for *Obedience* with Milgram as their author in mind. The notes focus primarily on the degree to which the subjects *performed* obedience or resistance. They privilege obedient subjects who demonstrated considerable tension. Despite the film's title, there were only four obedient subjects. Milgram wavered over which of these four men to feature as *the* obedient subject. Participants in the experiments were given a number to conceal their identities; the first part of the number referred to the version of the experiment (version 25 for the film), and the second part to its running order. Milgram did not use those numbers in his viewing notes. Instead, participants were referred to according to which reel of film they appeared in and its running order. Initially, I tried to match the subject records with the parade of faces that appeared on film. In the outtakes, fourteen men appeared on-screen—some for lengthy periods, others just a glimpse. The subject records noted the starting time of each participant's session. I arranged them chronologically, from the evening of Friday, May 25, through to Sunday, May 27. As with so many other aspects of this experiment, it was not as orderly as the reported procedures and statistics implied. While I could match most of the faces in the unreleased footage to their subject records, there were a few anomalies.

Subject 2505 was quickly removed from consideration. His performance at the shock machine was "not very convincing or interesting." Subject 2504 was under consideration from the beginning. An entire reel of film was devoted to his performance. Milgram recorded that the "subject is rather dumb." Subject 2504 turned toward the Experimenter and expressed concern. "Not bad at all. It reeks of obedience . . . cringing look," Milgram wrote. The descriptions of the next section of footage were marked with an asterisk. Despite his obvious excitement about 2504's performance, Milgram also had some misgivings. Subject 2504 showed "tremendous ambivalence accepting the situation as genuine." While he could be used as *the* obedient subject, Milgram mused that a really genuine subject would be much better.

A third participant, who appeared at the beginning of reel 4, was also considered for *the* featured obedient subject. This was most likely 2509, whose footage Milgram marked as excellent. His performance was convincing, and there was an *excellent* buildup of tension and an *excellent* sense of obedience. He demonstrated just how difficult it was to stop. Viewing reel 5, Milgram was excited too. There was "a very good obedient subject" who held his hand over his mouth, laughed with his belly, and resisted strongly. This man's performance was brilliant. "Complete abdication," noted Milgram.[26] This subject was most likely 2512. According to written comments made during his session, 2512 laughed often. A snippet of the filmed outtakes show a middle-aged man in a suit who participated at approximately the right time on the right day. He complies with the Experimenter's instructions, smiling as he turns toward him. Was this the "complete abdication to authority" to which Milgram referred? There is very little surviving footage of this subject, so it was hard to make a call. However, as it happened, 2512 was out of the picture. What happened with 2509?

In a scene from *Northside 777*, James Stewart's character is unable to sleep. His investigation has hit some hurdles. His wife finds him in the living room gazing at an incomplete 500-piece jigsaw. McNeal speaks first, then his wife:

Let's work this out together.
What's the matter? Won't the pieces fit?
Some of them. But they make the wrong picture.
Pieces never make the wrong picture. Maybe you're looking at them from
the wrong angle.[27]

I returned to the archival materials and approached things from another direction. The first phase of editing *Obedience* selected key subjects based on performance. Completed by September 1962, the assembly edit ran at fifty minutes. Milgram noted that the order of some subjects should be swapped, the film should be shorter, and narration was needed. The documentary was put aside for some time as he settled into a new academic position at Harvard and sought further funding. Chris Johnson, a graduate student, began the second phase of editing in consultation with his former lecturer. An audiotape from the editing stage of the project was labeled "Instructions to Filmmaker." Could it be a voice memo? After first listening to it, I put it aside because it did not seem to reveal any new information. Later, though, I realized it was an audio copy of the assembly edit. I had been so fixated on visual evidence that I missed a vital piece of documentation right in front of me. I listened again. There was one obedient subject who does not appear in the completed film. He sounded distressed as he tried to get the Experimenter to stop, as is clear from the following excerpt from an audiotape labeled "Instructions to Filmmaker":

UNIDENTIFIED MAN: I have to give you 360 [volts].
[The sound of the buzzer as he inflicts a shock.]
[Silence.]
UNIDENTIFIED MAN: He's not responding. I want to know if this man is all right. I mean, I'll do it. I want to know if he's all right.
EXPERIMENTER: The experiment requires that you continue, Teacher.
UNIDENTIFIED MAN: Well, I'm sorry. I mean, I want you to check on this man . . .

I placed a snippet of the Unidentified Man's audio against images of each of the fourteen participants in the unreleased footage. A series of marks from the white chinagraph pencils editors once used indicated film that had been cut. When I placed the dialogue from the audiotape alongside unreleased film footage of 2509, they matched. There was another means of cross-checking. According to a note on his file, 2509 checked his watch as he worked his way up the shock machine. It was not always easy to see 2509's wrists because he wore a long-sleeved business shirt. I rewound the video in slow motion. Sure enough, as 2509 turned to the Experimenter, I saw a glimpse of his watch. Subject 2509 was the person under consideration, along with 2504, as *the* featured obedient subject. If my assumptions were correct, 2509 was removed from the film during the second phase of editing. Milgram was eager to reduce the film's length, and 2509's performance was less dramatic than that of other subjects.

Once the featured obedient subject was selected, the editing at Harvard continued with the further shaping of performances and the addition of new layers to construct an argument of "obedience to authority" as the default setting for humanity. However, a different argument could have been constructed from the unedited footage and subject records, since only four of

fourteen participants were recorded as fully obedient in the film version. The new
material included inserts of the shock machine with film noir–style lighting,
shots of Yale University, Milgram's narration, and credits. The latter all assist
in framing the documentary as scientific evidence—that is, data, not drama.
After time-consuming postproduction laboratory work, the documentary was
completed in 1965. Now that I knew *how* Milgram selected *Obedience*'s hyper-
obedient subject, I wanted to know more about *why*.

In a journal article published in 1965, the same year that the film was completed, Milgram quoted another obedient subject who was not associated with
any particular version of his experiment:

[150 volts delivered.] You want me to keep going?

[165 volts delivered.] That guy is hollering in there. There's a lot of them
here. He's liable to have a heart condition. You want me to go on?

[180 volts delivered.] He can't stand it! I'm not going to kill that man in
there! You hear him hollering? He's hollering. He can't stand it. What if something happens to him? . . .

This soon built to:

[240 volts delivered.] Aw no. You mean I've got to keep going up with the
scale? No sir. I'm not going to kill that man! I'm not going to give him 450
volts! [The Experimenter says, "The experiment requires that you go on."] I
know it does, but that man is hollering there, sir.[28]

In the story told by Milgram's data, participants were classified simply as
"obedient" or "disobedient." However, these scores did not convey the character of the subjects' performances fully, wrote the psychologist. They did not
convey the tension and emotional strain many participants experienced.
Deeply conflicted, participants were observed to "sweat, tremble, stutter, bite
their lips, and groan." Smiling and nervous laughter that seemed completely
inappropriate was also frequently observed. A small percentage of people had
uncontrollable laughing seizures, and on one occasion the experiment had to
be stopped. Transcripts were a better indication of mood than numbers, Milgram concluded, quoting from the above transcript. Its participant began the
experiment calmly but became increasingly tense and agitated.[29] This transcript matches that of 2504, the man assigned a leading role as *the* obedient
subject in *Obedience* and later featured in Milgram's book, where he was given
the pseudonym "Fred Prozi." Over time, an obedient documentary participant
became the Everyman of the entire series of experiments.

PERFORMANCE

According to documentary theorist Bill Nichols, the line between performance in fiction and documentary is relatively straightforward. In fiction, we simply ask the *actors* (who have entered a contractual agreement with the filmmakers) to do what we want. Directors have the right to elicit a suitable performance, and the actor's work is evaluated on the quality of the performance delivered rather than fidelity to their everyday behavior. By contrast, in documentary, *social actors* attempt to conduct their lives as they would without the presence of the camera. Their performances are valued according to the degree to which they embody or report on their own lives.[30] Social actors often stand in for the communities to which they belong. Accordingly, the *Obedience* documentary participants were *social actors*. Their performances were unrehearsed and captured via concealed cameras. They were unaware of being filmed until Milgram revealed that fact in postexperiment interviews.

There are closer parallels between fiction and nonfiction filmmaking in shaping recorded performances. In their guide to cross-cultural documentary production, Ilisa Barbash and Lucien Taylor observed that "documentary conventions of character development over the course of a film are uncannily close to fictional ones."[31] Documentary filmmakers often favor people whose behavior in front of the camera conveys the sense of complexity and depth we value in a trained actor's performance.[32] These observations strongly resonate with my experience as a director working across documentary and drama. I would add, though, that what is judged as a "good" performance may be a myriad of things depending on the era, culture, media, genre, and other factors. Fred Prozi's documentary performance was a good match with the highly naturalistic performances much lauded in postwar American fiction cinema and, in particular, the acting style that came to be known as the "American Method."

Following the 1920s tour of the Moscow Art Theatre—cofounded by Constantin Stanislavsky—two of his former students migrated to the United States, where they taught his acting method at the American Laboratory. Although his approach varied across his career, Stanislavsky was acclaimed for devising a system of acting that called on the actor to draw on their inner life. Actors were advised to build a sequence of interior images to illuminate their characters, "unfurling the roll of inner film" in each performance. Repeated projection would help them fill in the details that would keep the performance alive.[33] Guided by the search for truthfulness and rhythm, actors should work to their own *inner beat*. Lee Strasberg, Stella Adler, and Sanford Meisner, who worked together with the Group Theatre in the 1930s, adapted Stanislavsky's system. Although Stanislavsky's system was initially designed for the stage, it was frequently adopted for the screen. "The Method" reached the heights of its popularity in the 1950s and 1960s due to the Broadway and Hollywood success of actors such as Montgomery Clift, Marlon Brando, and Paul Newman. In the Cold War period, stripped of its Russian legacy, it was claimed as a distinctively American method. As theater historian Bruce McConchie wrote, during the Cold War, there was a great deal of social anxiety about what was genuine and what was fabricated.[34] The American Method appeared to result in displays of genuine behavior and emotions.

Prozi was particularly expressive on-screen. He revealed considerable inner conflict, leaning in, turning, jumping to his feet, pacing, remonstrating with the Experimenter, and sighing. In addition to his performance at the shock machine, Prozi's behavior in his debrief with Stanley Milgram made for compelling viewing. "Why didn't you stop?" Milgram asked Prozi immediately afterward. "I tried to make him stop," cried Prozi, "I tried." Small gestures often make a film performance—Prozi removed a pack of cigarettes from his trouser pocket, tapped one out and placed it in his mouth. Forgetting to light it, he removed the cigarette from his mouth and placed it back in again. As Milgram explained that no one was actually hurt, a mix of relief and concern crossed Prozi's face. Finally, he lit his cigarette. Taking a deep drag, he exhaled. (Those are the kind of moments at which audiences also often collectively breathe out.) McDonough playing the Victim, bounced across the room to shake hands. Prozi exclaimed, "Well, am I glad to see you, buddy!" His relief and delight were palpable. "Animated and *alive*" were the terms Milgram used to describe Prozi's performance.[35]

Sanford Meisner's version of the American Method emphasized listening, answering, and responding in the moment. Watching Prozi on-screen, I was struck by just how well he listened. In an extended close-up during the debrief, Prozi flexed his jaw as he tried to take in what he was hearing; he looked as if he might cry. Early in my filmmaking career, I was a trainee on the Australian television miniseries *Heroes* (1987). As the director shot one scene, I was asked to rehearse the next scene. The ensemble cast included the Australian actor John Hargreaves. It was more moving to watch someone trying *not* to express an emotion, he told me. That is one of the reasons that watching Fred Prozi listen to Stanley Milgram is so affecting. Prozi's performance is, in part, a documentary version of the kind of performances produced by professional actors trained in the American Method. It is accomplished not only through the selection and editing of the material but also through the rhythms inscribed on it during its staging and filming. Unlike the character description that Milgram later wrote, it conveys something of Prozi's inner life.

CHARACTER

In *Aspects of the Novel*, E. M. Forster distinguished between flat and rounded characters. The former are types often constructed around a single quality or idea. According to the novelist, flat characters are easily identified and remembered; however, only rounded characters are "ready for an extended life."[36] For Forster, whose categories were initially derived from drama, round characters always trump flat characters. Various nonfiction film theorists and writers of documentary production manuals have uncritically adopted Forster's "flat versus round" hierarchy of characters. Carl Plantinga, for example, suggests that most documentary characters are flat since there is rarely time to develop complexity.[37] Literary critic James Wood, however, offers some welcome new insights. Rejecting the divide between flat and round characters, Wood observes that "many so-called flat characters seem more *alive* to me, more interesting as human studies, however short-lived, than the round characters they are supposedly subservient to."[38] Moreover, a wide range of characters can be found in fiction: "There are thousands of different kinds of people, some round, some flat, some deep, some caricatures, some realistically evoked, some brushed with the lightest of strokes."[39] Narrative design, I would add, involves balancing different kinds of characters.

Stanley Milgram's book *Obedience to Authority* finally appeared in 1974, after a lengthy struggle to write about the events that had taken place in his psychology laboratory more than a decade earlier. Character was very much on his mind. Milgram's experience shaping his *Obedience* documentary laid the groundwork for the book, which was aimed at both an academic audience and a broader readership. Approximately a dozen participants from across all the versions of the experiments were featured. They were introduced via their character name, their occupation, and the version of the experiment in which they appeared. Participant 2504, for example, was "Fred Prozi, Unemployed" (in experiment 5). Thus, one of his defining characteristics was that he did not have a job. As his subject file records, "Fred Prozi" was from the wrong side of the tracks. Milgram provided the following character description: "The subject is about fifty years old, dressed in a jacket but no tie; he has a good natured, if slightly dissolute. appearance. He employs working class grammar and strikes one as a rather ordinary fellow."[40] The word *dissolute* in this account is particularly striking. It is frequently used to describe drunks—here, it implies a lack of morals.

Over time, the transcripts that Milgram prepared more closely resembled a script for film or television. By 1974, Prozi's transcript described him as yelling, screaming, and interrupting. By contrast, the Experimenter was described as patient and speaking with detached calm. Neither observation is entirely borne out by the archival materials. Also indicative of the greater drama that Milgram introduced into his transcripts of experimental sessions is the use of the term *electric chair* to describe the shock machine in Prozi's transcript.[41]

In the closing scenes of *Call Northside 777*, McNeal finally solves his puzzle. A lawyer asks him to go over his new evidence; they need hard facts. "OK I'll give you something better than the facts—a picture!" McNeal produces a photograph from his coat pocket with a flourish. But where is the documentation that provides context? Long before the advent of digital photography, it was widely understood that photographs alone, or films alone, could not provide firm evidence—data needed to be corroborated and contextualized. Because *Call Northside 777* is a Hollywood film, the puzzle is definitively solved. Real life, though, is rarely so black and white.

In addition to its narrative about visual evidence, *Call Northside 777* provides another element relevant to a discussion of *Obedience*. Like Tom Hanks now, James Stewart (often called Jimmy) spent much of his career playing charming, self-effacing Everymen. Director Henry Hathaway recalled that he cast Stewart in *Call Northside 777* due to the pleasant demeanor that formed part of his star persona: "I knew the audience would instantly identify with him because of his niceness."[42]

Semidocumentary noirs revolved around good, decent men who did their jobs well—police officers, lawyers, reporters, and taxmen. Their investigations were low-key and methodical. They could not be further removed from the Everyman crafted by Stanley Milgram, a dark presence in the nation's midst. One of the dramatic hooks that Milgram repeated from his pilot studies onward was this: should we wish to recruit personnel to operate death camps in the United States like those in Nazi Germany, there would be no shortage of takers in New Haven. Carl Plantinga argued that turning a participant into a character in the context of a documentary typically involves placing them in a moral or sociopolitical context that implies a judgment.[43] Fred Prozi, cast as the Everyman of *Obedience*, took the rap for an entire community, an entire nation.

"The movie people got it all wrong." Writer Maureen Howard reported her father saying this about *Boomerang* (1947), a semidocumentary noir based on an unsolved case. Like me, Howard is the daughter of a detective and preoccupied with postwar films that combine information, story, drama, and data. She wondered: How much did *Boomerang* resemble the real-life events it depicted? The novelist, whose father was a consultant on the film, launched her own reinvestigation. She searched legal and newspaper archives and, after amassing a mountain of evidence, realized she was looking for answers in all the wrong places. Audiences watched films like these with a double focus, following the investigation but always aware they were in the land of story. The search for authenticity was more important than definitive answers.[44]

I once thought we simply needed to change the story regarding Milgram's *Obedience*—construct a new narrative about the many participants who resisted orders to harm others. I would still like to re-edit Milgram's surviving footage and demonstrate how a film called *Disobedience* or *Resistance* could have been edited from the same materials—to place the photographic negative and positive side by side. (Indeed, I think this is entirely consistent with Milgram's own project and his stated desire to open his films to reinvestigation.) I no longer believe we simply need a different story; instead, we need more complex, nuanced stories to help us understand human behavior and more careful attention to the ethics of how those stories are constructed and reconstructed.

"I would like to mention one other thing. Is it all right if your performance is shown to other psychologists?" Milgram asked as he wrapped up his debrief with *Obedience*'s Everyman. "Is it OK with you?" "I would say so," answered a visibly chuffed Prozi.

Stanley Milgram, polite and courteous in the debriefs he conducted, appeared to do all he could to ensure Prozi left with his dignity intact. Milgram flattered him as he sought permission to use the footage. "You are an actor now. How do you feel about that?" he asked. The release form Prozi signed stated: "Any aspect of my performance in this experiment may be used freely for the purpose of scientific communication, whether in the form of articles, books, films, or other documents without further consent on my part."[45]

The last reported sighting of "Fred Prozi" was on Friday, May 25, 1962, after he signed a film release before leaving Linsly-Chittenden Hall. The moon was waning, half its disk of light visible and the rest in shadow. It had been an unseasonably warm day. As he headed down High Street, dressed in dark slacks and a white polo shirt, Prozi would have made an easy target for anyone trailing him. Did he ever get another job? What did he make of his starring role in *Obedience* as it was screened around the world in the years to come? Did he ever see himself on film? After 9:53 P.M., the picture goes blank.

CHAPTER 3

New Haven Noir

Picture this. It is midevening on October 21, 1961. Looking down over New Haven, there are tree canopies dotting the landscape along with the buildings and spires of Yale University. We follow a beige car as it proceeds down Chapel Street, turns right, and passes under the High Street Bridge. Adorned with angels and gargoyles, the bridge acts as a symbolic crossing between town and campus. I imagine the vehicle as a Plymouth, a popular and serviceable American car of its era. At the wheel is a man in his late thirties, known to us only as Mr. 501. At his side is his wife, Mrs. 501, about whom we know even less. The car pulls up outside the imposing Linsly-Chittenden Hall. Only a few windows are lit. In the distance, the bells of Harkness Tower mark the hour. It is 9:00 P.M. Perhaps we hear a car door slamming before Mr. 501 makes his way inside. He has been invited to participate in Stanley Milgram's experiment, which he has been told is about learning and memory. Mrs. 501 is not invited—women are not being recruited.[1] Perhaps, as Mrs. 501 waits, she switches on the overhead light, checks the letter in her handbag, and wonders, "What in the world are they doing in there?"

In an archive, each researcher constructs their own trail of evidence. Over the course of nearly a decade, I made several trips to view the Stanley Milgram Papers archived at Yale University—sometimes for months at a time. I ordered files and recordings online. (In this account, I have combined the various trips for clarity.) The *Obedience* documentary led me to participants' individual subject records and then to box 44.[2] The latter contained more than 600 responses to a questionnaire Milgram sent out a year after his experiments wrapped. The comments were typed onto index cards and coded before being placed in a box. Subsequently, the most troubled participants were identified and invited to small group discussions. The recordings of those sessions and transcripts were placed in box 155.[3] I began chasing "persons of interest" through the mass of files, recordings, and computer printouts, compiling dossiers on individual subjects.

In the words of psychiatrist and writer Peter Kramer, "Whilst data are important, numbers can imply an order to events that is misleading. Stories are better at capturing a different type of big picture."[4] A method long used by screenwriters involves writing out individual scenes on index cards and color-coding key characters or story strands. When the project has built sufficient momentum, the writer lays out the cards on a table, ordering and reordering them until, as with a jigsaw puzzle, a picture begins to fall into place. As a filmmaker, I could not help seeing those hundreds of typed cards and documents as a collective story waiting to be told.

The first-person accounts were vivid, as if warm hues had been added to a black-and-white film. Participants wrote as if they had been cast in a film noir narrative. According to Milgram, his "Obedience to Authority" experiments were inspired by the murder of more than 6 million Jews in the Holocaust. Why did so many ordinary people join in? He set out to investigate. A number of the New Haven participants' stories began with a suspected murder. A man held in a basement was being harmed. What had actually happened? Who was responsible? Others reported waiting outside the laboratory for the Experimenter and Teacher to emerge and tailing them through the Yale University campus at night—driving home, gazing into the beam of headlights on the road, and trying to make sense of a glimpse of a man putting on his hat and disappearing through a doorway. The click of a reel-to-reel recorder crossfading with the sound of a siren in the distance. Talking with their spouses late into the night. Checking the death notices for weeks to come. The whole town was talking.

On the eve of shooting an independent feature film in 2002, and suffering from the filmmaker's version of stage fright, I bought a copy of psychologist Jerome Bruner's *Making Stories*.[5] I packed the slim volume into my on-set bag as a talisman—to remind me that not all stories resembled the three-act structure touted by then Hollywood guru Syd Field and others. Stories were not fixed but living organisms. Bruner considered how we make sense of our lives through stories. In one investigation, he asked people to give an account of their lives in half an hour. Sifting through their stories, Bruner found people composed them by drawing on various structures borrowed from music, literature, and drama: from classical music's variations on a theme to literature's bildungsroman or existential novel. Stories often played out as scenes. Place played a critical role. We carried maps in our heads of both home and "the world out there." Autobiographical storytellers shifted between passive and active voices, flashed back to the past, and, just as often, flashed forward to possible selves. Language often turned inward as they considered moral dilemmas. Key images could shape a life story. Repeated phrases could become refrains. The way we tell stories lays down pathways to structuring experience. Bruner concluded that we do not simply tell stories about our world; rather, the stories we tell shape that world.

Making Stories proved a useful companion, and Bruner's writings led me to the work of sociologist Arthur Frank. Negotiating a health crisis, Frank began studying illness narratives and discovered that different kinds of stories contained distinct aspects of his experience. In turn, they connected him to different communities. The sociologist launched into a broader investigation of the capacities and dangers of stories. Stories, argued Frank, are the medium through which we learn who we are, who we are in relationship to those around us, and how we should behave in various scenarios. Stories locate us in relation to others. They not only bring us together but also can drive us apart. The bedrock of stories available to any community can include folktales and fables, legends and parables, urban myths, and tales drawn from literature and popular culture. On narrative resources, Arthur Frank said, "People tell their own unique stories, but they compose stories by adapting and combining narrative types that cultures make available."[6] Rather than ready-made, off-the-shelf templates, stories are improvised from the materials at hand.

In Connecticut in the 1960s, courtroom drama was a widely available genre. The trial of Adolf Eichmann, one of the first major television events, was broadcast live in 1961 as a season-length morality play. The Eichmann trial was filmed with concealed cameras, and director Leo Hurwitz edited live feeds from the four cameras to compile the highlights programs flown to the United States and Europe for broadcast each evening. Some of the most striking images of those broadcasts are close-ups of Eichmann, who sat inside a bulletproof capsule and consequently became known as "The Man in the Glass Booth." Time and time again, the coverage shifts to Eichmann, who chose to wear an ill-fitting suit rather than his Nazi uniform. He polished his glasses. He shuffled papers while witnesses gave their evidence. Those pictures were some of the first to come to mind for many people when news broke of Milgram's experiments. Some people asked themselves: Were they like Eichmann? Or even worse? After reading Milgram's long-awaited report, one participant's wife exclaimed, "Call yourself 'Eichmann'!"

The Eichmann trial was not the only courtroom drama showing in New Haven. A photograph of a local movie theater, taken just as the "Obedience" experiments began, depicts light spilling from streetlights to form star-shaped patterns against the night sky. Marquee signs announce Spencer Tracy in *Judgement in Nuremberg*.[7] The Academy Award–winning movie, based on a television script, dramatized one of the trials held by the Allies in 1947. Examining collective guilt, it presented some of the actual footage shot by the Allies when the Nazi concentration camps were liberated. Director Stanley Kramer cast stars in even minor roles, aiming to ensure the film's box office success. Spencer Tracy was brought out of retirement to play the American judge who presided over the trial. As he prepares to summarize the proceedings, the frail actor momentarily closes his eyes as if overcome by emotion. We can only imagine the full horror of the evidence presented. Tracy launches into his summation: "This trial has shown that under a national crisis, ordinary, even able and extraordinary men, can delude themselves into the commission of crimes so vast and heinous that they beggar the imagination." Was that not the dramatic premise underlying Milgram's experiment playing out down the road in his purpose-built Yale Interaction Laboratory?

People were more likely to be influenced by legal shows on television than they were by movies depicting those on trial for crimes against humanity. Created by lawyer-turned-novelist Erle Stanley Gardner, the *Perry Mason* series was required viewing from 1957 to 1966.[8] The fictional lawyer was defined by his sense of justice and basic faith in humanity. Everyone, it seemed, was now an investigator or a courtroom critic. A legal counselor who participated in Milgram's experiments went into the local courthouse on the weekend and tried to trace the Victim. He wanted to phone the man and check on his health. Another participant who described his occupation as "private police work" made his own inquiries. How could Yale University possibly do this to people? The residents of Connecticut did not want to simply watch *Perry Mason*. They wanted to *be* Perry Mason.

"It's all done with mirrors." This was the explanation my father, a detective, gave to my siblings and me when he had had enough of our endless questions. However, the "Obedience" experiments were literally conducted with mirrors. The two-way mirror that looked onto his basement laboratory enabled Milgram to observe experimental sessions without participants' knowledge. Further, later, it was from behind a two-way mirror in room 107 of Linsly-Chittenden Hall that he watched group debriefs conducted by a Yale University psychiatrist. A two-way mirror, coated with approximately half the reflective particles of a conventional mirror, usually divides two spaces. The observation area is dimly lit while the performance space beckons brightly. Raise the house lights, though, and the artifice is revealed.

If I were to give this New Haven noir story a name, I would borrow *Murderers amongst Us*—the proposed title for émigré director Fritz Lang's *M*.[9] Made in Germany in the early 1930s, *M* was the story of a town's hunt to track down a serial child murderer. Many of Lang's story lines were plucked from newspaper headlines. In the unsettled period in Germany that followed World War I, including the collapse of the economy, widespread unemployment, and the rise of fascism, there were several mass murderers. Lang, an avid reader, followed key cases. He spoke with police about their investigation techniques, examined their files, and consulted with psychiatrists and psychoanalysts. *M* would explore the idea that "any of us might turn into a murderer in exceptional circumstances." This dramatic premise also underlies the *Obedience* scenarios.

The books of French writer Patrick Modiano were also on my must-read list. Browsing in a bookshop, I picked up a copy of his novel *Missing Persons*.[10]

A private detective, trying to solve the mystery of his own past, sought clues in the shadowy streets of Paris. Modiano's detective, converting scraps of paper and scrawled numbers into investigative leads, spoke to me. I, too, endlessly walked the streets in search of evidence—unfortunately, the streets of New Haven rather than Paris. What mystery was I trying to solve? Were Milgram's participants the missing persons I was attempting to trace? Recalling my detective father's advice, I wrote out an index card and slipped it in my notebook: "stick to the facts."

In the spring of 1963, Stanley Milgram asked psychiatrist Paul Errera to run debrief sessions for his most troubled subjects in an attempt to ensure that no one suffered long-term harm.[11] Additionally, Milgram hoped to elicit individual stories for the book he was struggling to write. As collaborators, the two men were well matched. High achievers, both were appointed to positions at Yale University at a relatively young age. From Jewish backgrounds, their families had fled Hungary and Belgium, respectively, in the 1930s. In the shadow of the Holocaust, Milgram staged dramas in his laboratory. Dr. Errera, who ran psychiatric clinics for war veterans, saw the long-term fallout of war at closer quarters. Long after the event, his patients presented with vaguely articulated symptoms that were difficult to shake.

Thought to be the first psychologist to use the term *debrief*, Milgram adapted a process pioneered by the U.S. military.[12] The practice was devised by Brigadier General S.L.A. Marshall, an official historian during World War II. After a major battle, Marshall gathered his troops together, and everyone was invited to describe their experience in as much detail as possible. Rank was temporarily suspended as a story was constructed in strict chronological order. Marshall called his method, which led to unusually vivid accounts of battles, historical group debriefing. An unexpected side effect was soon observed—soldiers who participated suffered less psychological damage than those who did not. Consequently, debriefing was gradually extended to psychological experiments, although with one significant difference: unlike in historical group debriefing, power hierarchies and relationships stayed firmly in place during psychological experiment debriefs. Participants, called "subjects," were debriefed by experimenters. The latter chose what to reveal or not to reveal.

The two men began by reviewing participants' responses to questionnaires that accompanied Milgram's report of his preliminary findings. He noted that most people obeyed seemingly legitimate authority figures, and most described themselves as being glad to have participated. A minority, though, was clearly concerned. These troubled souls were invited to attend the small-group discussions held each Thursday over the dinner hour. It was not the most convenient time, but it was the only gap Errera had in his crowded schedule. I read the transcripts in box 155, trying to envisage how individuals might have delivered each line. Drawing on his clinical skills, Errera elicited participants' accounts. Individual narratives began to mesh with an emerging collective story. However, not everyone was willing to be guided toward the authorized version of the story that their facilitator seemed to have in mind. Those who could not let the anguished cries of the Victim fade from memory could not let the experimenters off the hook.

Many saw the experiment as a test of character. "I would like to know as an individual how I scored," asked one. "I should like any additional reports you may issue so that I may analyze my actions and reactions to this test more clearly," requested another. "I guess the test proves that I am naïve," a man concluded. One subject, a Yale University professor, was adamant that he did not want any information on the subject of where he broke off (i.e., refused to continue administering shocks to the Victim) compared with where someone else broke off. He would have liked to have stopped earlier. "I can identify a kind of guilt there," he said. "I don't feel pleased about that and I don't want to know anything more about it." He felt he had failed a moral test.

On February 28, 1963, eight subjects classified as "obedient" attended one of the first discussions.[13] The group debriefs often began with uneasy jokes. Were the experimenter and psychiatrist leveling with the subjects? Or had they been set up? An exchange between Dr. Errera and subjects in another group session began in a lighthearted manner:

"We realized from the letter that it was all rigged," said one participant.
Errera tried to clarify. "All of you have gone through the same kind or a variation of the same——."
"No paid actors," interrupted another participant.
"Just the doctor," quipped someone else.
"This part is not rigged but you're being recorded," replied Errera.

Participants in the session with defiant participants conducted on March 14, 1963, began with some of the same uneasy observations.

"I assume everything we say here is taped," said one.
"You serious?" someone else responded.
"Everything is recorded. Dr. Milgram is somewhere outside here but I think he is just making sure the tapes are working," said Errera.[14]

"More gestapo," participant 03XX quipped. Later, he elaborated on the theme: "My first reaction stepping into the room was that this was a gestapo-like surrounding like one sees in the movies or television. . . . I could see this battery of lights and buttons and shock." It is worth noting that prisoner-of-war and escape movies were some of the staples of postwar cinema in the United States and Britain.

In a conversation with Milgram, Errera identified one of the obedient subjects as the most disturbed. He believed the man he had shocked was probably dead when he opened the door. Yet, he said, "I felt nothing, it didn't bother me, I did my job." It spooked the psychiatrist. By contrast, Milgram found it a fascinating insight, so much so that he selected the man as a key case study for his book, giving him the alias of "Pasqual Gino, water inspector."[15] Treating Milgram's index cards and transcripts simply as data to be quantified, it is easy to take Gino's comments at face value. However, his files provide more context and suggest a different story.[16] Forty-three years old and married, Gino was a fireman who lived in the neighboring town of Hamden. He described his great relief at receiving the preliminary report of Milgram's findings and attributed his behavior to having served in the military during World War II: "When the lieutenant says you're going to crawl on your gut, you crawl on your gut." Yet one chilling detail emerges from his records. More than seventeen years after being discharged from the armed forces, Gino was still receiving psychiatric treatment at the local veterans hospital. This fact puts a different slant on his insistence that he was "happy to have been of service." Should the war veteran not have been screened out of the experiment?

Much ink has been spilled describing and debating shades of film noir. In 1946, Italian screenwriter and critic Nino Frank sat down to watch American movies that had been unavailable during the war. Across the Atlantic, they were making a new kind of police drama, he observed. People had a hunger for reality. "We've become familiar with the formula for detective stories: an unsolved crime, some suspects, and in the end the discovery of a guilty party through the diligence of an experienced observer."[17] Following the war, audiences were far more interested in how people behaved under pressure rather than questions of "who done it." Film noir was not terribly invested in plot or action. Instead, it focused on the psychology of criminals and the "facial expressions, gestures, and utterances" that revealed character.[18]

Decades later, American writer and director Paul Schrader penned his own "Notes on Noir." Borrowing from many sources, including German expressionism, the gangster film, and poetic realism, noir depicted a world of dark, slick city streets, crime, and corruption, said Schrader. Noir embraced mood and atmosphere. Nighttime streets glistened with freshly fallen rain. Actors delivered their lines standing in the shadows.[19] As one filmmaker said, "The night ruled in film noir, the shadow more important than the light."[20] In *Blackout*, film historian Sheri Biesen makes a case for two phases of film noir: wartime and postwar. The latter style reflected Cold War anxieties, including organized crime, the rise of communism, and the atomic bomb. Good and evil were no longer so clear-cut, and the deep blacks and harsh shadows of earlier film noir gave way to shades of gray. Anxiety and paranoia, though, remained the order of the day.[21]

Winfried Fluck challenged the notion that film noir can be reduced to a set of endlessly repeated formulas or elements that must be included. He suggested that the term encompasses a wide range of films that share an atmosphere rather than a narrative pattern. Film noirs immerse us in the world of the night. For Fluck, guilt is one of the preoccupations of noir—specifically, the guilt of the citizen-turned-criminal. His account of film noir places questions of moral responsibility and the puzzle of criminal motivation in center frame.[22]

Day after day in New Haven, I arrived at the archives at opening time and left at closing time, blinking as I emerged into the early evening. As I stepped from interior lighting to twilight, I walked down Hilltop Avenue, lined with historic mansions and sweeping driveways. I gazed in at lit windows and imagined people sitting down to dinner and conversation before resuming my walk toward the bed-and-breakfast where I was staying. I registered the Stars and Stripes flying in support of the U.S. military's latest Middle East mission as I turned the front door key in its lock. I listened to the echo of my footsteps as I made my way down empty hallways, sensing muffled voices and movements behind doorways. Separated from my partner and our daily routines in Sydney, I began to feel unmoored. Day after day in the archive, I read accounts of fear and paranoia—a place where nothing was quite as it seemed. Constant warnings from the university police about where it was safe to walk in New Haven, reportedly one of the most violent cities in America, only added to my unease. Anxiety consumed me. Is all this strictly relevant? Possibly—no, make that probably. Ivan Jablonka advocated creative history as a process in which every aspect of an investigation is made transparent—temporal and imaginative journeys, following up leads, scrutinizing documents, interrogating witnesses, and choosing the right words and images to fashion a text.[23] Such a process can extend to noting one's preoccupations and state of mind. It is all part of the investigation. I began to feel as though I was in a film noir myself.

On March 21, 1963, the spring equinox in the Northern Hemisphere, the hours of daylight and dark were roughly equal. In New Haven on that day, the sun rose at approximately 7:00 A.M. and set at 7:00 P.M. As families gathered around the dinner table, Mr. and Mrs. 501 drove to Yale University from Guilford—a distance of approximately seventeen miles. Mr. 501, who took the wheel, had been invited to a gathering to rehash his experiences. Mrs. 501 was not invited. Nevertheless, she decided to accompany him—again. What do we know about this couple? I consulted Mr. 501's subject record.[24] All we know of Mrs. 501 is what we can glean from her husband's file. She, like most of the wives of male participants, is one of the missing persons of this story. In October 1961, when his experimental session was held, Mr. 501 was thirty-eight years old and employed as a clerk at a local plumbing supply store. During four years of military service, Mr. 501 reached the rank of petty officer second class but did not serve overseas. Born in Connecticut and affiliated with the Congregational Church, Mr. 501 was one of four siblings. There is no record of whether he and his wife had children of their own.

As a filmmaker, I found myself visualizing some of the key events I read about in transcripts. In that liminal space between day and night, as the light fades and streetlights are switched on, Mrs. 501 waits in the car. This time, though, something propels her inside. She makes her way up the stairs and through the building's main entrance. Perhaps she glances around to take in the marble floors and wood-paneled walls before muffled voices lead her to room 107. I envisage her hesitating at the door before creeping in. Several men, including her husband, are gathered in a small seminar room. Unbeknownst to Mrs. 501, Milgram busies himself with the tape recorder behind the two-way mirror. Dr. Errera invites Mrs. 501 to join them. "I just came in from the car to get out of the cold," she says before taking a seat at the edge of the group.[25] Later, the psychiatrist may well have regretted offering that invitation.

"Your neighbor could be the murderer," the anxious townspeople are told in Lang's *M*. In one early scene, after receiving a tip the police raid an apartment. A woman protests as the officer rifles through drawers and cupboards. Her husband is a model citizen. She exclaims: "Searching an honest man's flat because of an anonymous letter!" "Calm down," the officer replies, "we are only doing our duty." The guilty man had left no trace. No one appeared to know anything. And yet, "he was one of us." They must follow every lead, interrogate every man on the street.[26] We come back to this idea again and again. An inspector tells the crowd that any one of them could be the culprit.

One participant from the "Pressure to Obey" version of the experiment caught my attention. He was among the small group of defiant subjects invited to a symposium held on April 11, 1963.[27] The bare facts were these. Aged thirty-nine and married, the subject was a purchasing manager in the fashion industry. Born in New York to parents who had migrated from Russia and Poland, respectively, he served in the armed forces during World War II and was an alderman on the New Haven City Council.[28] How did he tell his story? One documentary noir variant involved an investigation by concerned public officials. The alderman's account matches that template. He arrived home on the night in question and talked over his concerns with his wife. The alderman vowed that he would not rest until he got to the bottom of the matter. The next day, he called the Yale University psychology department. He consulted with other men he knew who had participated and called Milgram. However, this is where the alderman's account departs from the familiar pattern. He found himself blocked at every turn. There was no systematic investigation undertaken by local authorities that aimed to get to the bottom of things. In fact, the university was part of the problem.

The alderman ramped up his inquiries. A young woman in his office had spoken with several participants. Most of them inflicted the maximum shocks. They were no better than the people who ran concentration camps during the war, she said. On a business trip to New York, the alderman discussed the experiment with close friends. One of them, a Holocaust survivor, was married to a

United Nations official. Hearing about the trials being conducted in New Haven, she was very upset. How could experiments like those the Nazis conducted in concentration camps be run in Connecticut? Should the United Nations be informed?

Who was the suspect in this New Haven noir? Theories varied. Some had their suspicions about the experimenters. Other subjects worried about neighbors and workmates. Exactly how many people were in on this thing? For others, the stuff of nightmares was even closer to home. What had they got themselves caught up in? Goethe wrote that every man carried around a secret that would horrify his neighbor. Had they—however unwittingly—killed a man? What was really happening down at Yale University? Who was responsible? Why was there a cover-up?

Now, picture this. Mrs. 501 stayed at the edge of the group, listening. The conversation soon turns to her husband. He was distressed that he had continued to shock a man despite his loud protests. No matter how many times Mr. 501 went over the event, he could not picture the Victim getting out of the chair: "He was dead. . . . I was completely convinced that he was getting the shock. I was giving him that shock. I was shaken." Mrs. 501 confirmed her husband's emotional state: "He was completely shaken." The couple were soon co-narrating their story. If there is one thing that Milgram's experiments demonstrate, it is this—the state of many marriages in New Haven at that time was rock solid. Participant after participant recalled going home and discussing the event with their wife long into the night. Mrs. 501 continued, "I was shivering. I was parked out in front. It was cold. I thought, 'what in the world are they doing in there?'"[29]

Once again, Errera guided the discussion toward the participant's personal responsibility for his actions. How did Mr. 501 feel knowing that he was capable of killing a man? Mrs. 501 interjected. Perhaps, behind his two-way mirror, Stanley Milgram leaned forward, listened more carefully. Her husband was very upset by the experience because he had never hurt anyone. During World War II, Mr. 501 had not seen combat. The only possible explanation for her husband continuing was that he had made an agreement with the experimenter: "I'm talking as—not as his wife, no sir. I couldn't, I mean I—when he got in the car I said, 'well that's absolutely ridiculous.'" The transcriber underlined those words to convey the force with which Mrs. 501 spoke.[30]

Reading the transcripts, I imagine doing a cut and paste of the dialogue and rehearsing the scenes with actors. I do not have access to the original audiotapes, only the words on the page, and much of the context has been edited out: tone of voice, rhythms of speech, overlaps and interruptions, gaps, and silences—all are absent. I envisage different 'line readings.' Did Mrs. 501 get under Errera's skin? Or did Errera manage to maintain his professional demeanor?

The Stanley Milgram Papers make detectives of us all—no coincidence given the collection's rich depository of materials and still extremely relevant questions.

A born-and-bred New Haven private investigator reported that he had obeyed the Experimenter all the way to the end (i.e., administered the maximum voltage shock to the Victim) but was extremely upset by his actions. He considered going to Yale University and making inquiries of his own. How could they allow such a thing? Now there was a story! There were traces of information in the Stanley Milgram Papers that could turn into viable leads everywhere—details of participants' age, marital status, employment history, and ethnic background— names and addresses (accidentally) not redacted. Some participants have long ago publicly identified themselves. Working with archival documents requires special attention to details that may have been overlooked, checking and cross-checking to flush out new information. But which clues should be followed up?

In some cases, after many painstaking hours, I matched redacted records of participants with the individuals concerned. What are the ethics of revealing this information? Should I approach the families and descendants of those concerned? I struggled with this question before approaching it from a different direction. Writing about cold cases, criminologist Ron Mendall noted that every investigation requires a working theory. Why has the case been reopened? Without a clear answer, an investigation is stuck at the "spinning wheels" stage.[31] My focus was this: How did participants draw on narrative resources to make sense of their experiences? I concluded that identifying individuals lay outside my brief.

Of the dozens of accounts I read from box 155, it was the story of Mr. and Mrs. 501 that claimed me. I was moved by Mrs. 501's tenacity. Protective of her husband and his fragile mental state, she was determined to get to the bottom of things. Routinely not invited to participate in gatherings and events on account of her gender, she simply invited herself and proceeded to conduct her own investigation. I delved further into the files, incomplete as they were. Drawing on transcripts and records, I visualized the scene.

Exterior. Road. Night. We follow Mr. and Mrs. 501 as they drive home around 10:00 P.M. on Tuesday, October 12, 1961. It was a foggy night. Visibility was poor. They most likely took the back route home to Guilford. Mrs. 501 asks if she should drive. Rejecting her offer, Mr. 501 takes the wheel. There are not that many ways to shoot driving scenes. In my film version, the camera would be rigged on a vehicle traveling ahead, looking back at Mr. and Mr. 501 and holding them in a two-shot. The amber light of the dashboard illuminates their faces. As Mr. 501 gradually regains control of his emotions, his story spills out. It all started innocently enough. He was given a series of instructions and a sample shock. He did a practice run of reading out the word pairs. Less than twenty minutes later, he found himself pushing a button to inflict high-voltage shocks on a man who cried out about a heart condition. Mr. 501 pushed the button until he was told to stop. Another human being might now be dead due to his actions.[32] Mrs. 501 can scarcely believe what she is hearing. The beam of their headlights barely cuts through the fog. Cocooned in the car, the couple keep rehashing the events of the evening as they try to make sense of it all.

In room 107, Errera suggested that the alderman recount his experience in less dramatic terms. Did he feel that he had gone too far? That even a few shocks were too many? "If there was *any* element of hurting people, physically hurting people, it [the experiment] should be stopped," the alderman insisted. Perhaps the elected public official would have found the experience easier to live with if he rehearsed a different way of telling his story. But he felt a responsibility to family, workmates, political and religious affiliations, and the broader community. Errera's authorized version robs the alderman and other New Haven residents of agency. To whom was the psychiatrist responsible? The participants? Or the experimenter?

Postwar Hollywood was enamored of all things related to psychology and psychiatry.[33] There were stories of psychiatrists who suffered breakdowns or were imposters and doubles, along with a grab bag of related imagery, including lie detectors and mirrors. This may have partly been due to leading directors, including Alfred Hitchcock and Billy Wilder, having served in psychological warfare units during World War II. The films they produced included newsreels showing the atrocities uncovered when the Allies liberated Nazi concentration camps. There was concern that the public would not believe the evidence. Consequently, Hitchcock was asked to consult on the British documentary *Memory of the Camps*.[34] Hitchcock advised using graphics to show each of the eleven concentration camps in its geographic context. Where were the nearest villages? Who lived there? How many ordinary people must have known of the existence of the camps?

Peter Lorre played the child murderer in *M*. Facing the court, his character confessed he had finally found the source of the darkness that haunted him. He walked the streets day and night, unable to shake the feeling that someone was following him, until eventually he realized, "It is I myself . . . following me." As Milgram's series of experiments drew to a close in January 1962, he struggled with his conscience. In notes he titled "An Experimenter's Dilemma," he outlined his personal quandary.[35] A man with a heart condition pleaded to be let out of an electric chair. The experimenter refused. Surely, this was unethical? Or, even worse, immoral? Subjects were deeply distressed. Why did he feel justified in continuing? The doubts kept coming. His findings could be used by those looking to elicit greater obedience. Personal ambition, rather than a desire to help mankind, was most likely his overriding motive: "When an investigator keeps his eyes open through a scientific study, he learns things about himself as well as his subjects and the observations do not always flatter."[36]

Individuals do not make up stories; rather, we all work with the narrative resources available to us. Stories are our companions, claims Arthur Frank. They can be helpful or dangerous.[37] As a genre, postwar documentary noir was particularly open to repurposing and adaptation since some of its key hallmarks were mood and atmosphere rather than plot.

That autumn in New Haven, I found myself drawn to the music of Estonian composer Arvo Pärt. I wanted to tune out some of the darkness. In midlife, Pärt rejected his artistic work to date and went into an exile he described as going deep into the shadows. He would make an artistic investigation. A few years later, the composer emerged with a new style inspired by the action of a bell as it moved from side to side. Pärt was interested in the spaces between the notes. Everything about his music spoke to me. I walked all over New Haven. This time, though, I left my research notes behind. I walked to concert halls, auditorium, and churches. It was Easter, and it seemed that Pärt's quiet meditative music was being rehearsed or played everywhere. As I crept into the performing spaces, large and small, I took my place alongside rows of people listening intently. There was the rustle of programs, someone trying to suppress a cough, a whisper fading away. We were together alone.

It is difficult to close this New Haven noir. I do not yet have the answers I am looking for. In the last decade or two, the files of Stanley Milgram have been reopened. (Perhaps they were never really closed?) Scores of researchers have pored over them as newly redacted materials come to light, new lines of inquiry are generated, and leads investigated and cross-checked. My own preliminary findings? The dossiers on individuals that I have compiled suggest a collective story: a counterinvestigation run by concerned citizens. They include Mr. and Mrs. 501, the alderman, a New Haven private detective, a legal counselor, a Yale University forestry professor, the local synagogue, and many others.

Imagine this. New Haven. A summer's night in early 1962. The forestry professor picks up the telephone. He dials a number and demands to speak with Stanley Milgram. The legal counselor breaks into the courthouse files, rifles through the records, one eye always on the door. The private detective stakes out Linsly-Chittenden Hall, records people entering and exiting, and sweeps his flashlight across the stairs to the basement. The alderman takes the train to New York. Light flickers behind a window. A group of concerned citizens gather at the local synagogue. Milgram must account for his actions. Mrs. 501, sitting in the Plymouth, is caught in the beam of a passing car's headlights. Their story is not about local participants as victims at the hands of an elite educational and research institution; rather, casting themselves as players in a documentary noir was a means of restoring agency to those disturbed by what may have been happening behind closed doors at Yale University.

CHAPTER 4

Good or Bad Samaritans?

In the early hours of March 13, 1964, New York City resident Catherine Geno-vese became the "Kitty Genovese" of a twentieth-century parable—social psychology's "Bystander Effect" experiment. Returning home late one night, twenty-eight-year-old Genovese was brutally raped and murdered outside her apartment on a quiet residential street. As detectives pursued her killer, a second line of investigation emerged. Thirty-eight local residents allegedly watched the tragic events unfold over an extended period but did nothing. These onlookers became "persons of interest" as a homicide investigation jump-started a broader inquiry into the behavior of people living in cities. Were we Bad Samaritans?

There were many versions of the Kitty Genovese story. However, it was the *New York Times* account of March 27, 1964, two weeks after the appearance of the newspaper's routine report of a murder, that shifted the focus of the investi-gation from the perpetrator to the onlookers. (By then, Winston Mosley had already confessed to the crime, plus the burglary, rape, and murder of another young woman, and was awaiting trial.) A global outpouring of concern and anger followed. The crime touched and continues to touch a social nerve. Two years later, a program of social psychology experiments initiated by John Darley and Bibb Latane sought explanations: Why did *so many* people ignore a dying woman? Were we Bad Samaritans? Another line of investigation by Irving and Jane Pilia-vin reported more Good Samaritans than have usually been recognized. The latter research failed to capture the public imagination in the same way. Why?

In the early 1990s, memory researcher John Kotre described social psychol-ogy experiments as "scientific parables."[1] Those that attracted the most atten-tion employed vivid imagery, conceptual simplicity, and story lines that led to a probing question. Stanley Milgram's *Obedience to Authority* was a good example. Experimental results were often counterintuitive. Most of Milgram's subjects were said to have gone all the way in inflicting harmful (ultimately fatal) shocks although it was predicted that only a tiny percentage would do so. Scientific parables also invited us to identify with the protagonist, who was usually the subject of the experiment: to ask ourselves, "What would *I* have done?" Psychology's parables were often linked to a signal crime or historical event—the Holocaust in the case of Milgram's *Obedience to Authority* and the murder of Kitty Genovese in the case of the bystander experiments. But what happens when experiments-as-parables are linked to factual accounts discovered to be incorrect? How do we separate the experiment and the event to create imaginative space to fashion new stories?

I delved into the newspaper archives to discover more about the Kitty Genovese story. I was not the first to do so, not by a long stretch. However, I wanted to trace its central dramatic image. That picture of thirty-eight witnesses watching from their lit windows at night played a leading role in imprinting the crime and the bystander experiments in the collective imagination, pulling focus from other stories and possible explanations.

In newspaper archives, I soon discovered *The Lonely Street*—the proposed film, that is. Within months of the Genovese killing, Warner Brothers purchased the rights to a story based on a "real-life murder witnessed by at least 38 witnesses."[2] "Genovese Slaying Script Sold," read one headline. Writer Harry Essex had managed to bash out a film treatment before the chalk marks at the crime scene (indicating a body) had faded. Essex began his career as a newspaper reporter in New York City and had some plays produced off Broadway. After he was discharged from the U.S. Army Signal Corps in 1947, the aspiring screenwriter found work in Hollywood. Essex soon racked up credits in comedy, science fiction, thrillers, and police procedurals. One way or another, he wrote—a lot. Essex's credits for films set on the dark side of the street included episodes of *The Untouchables* and additional dialogue for the landmark documentary film noir *He Walked by Night* (1948). The screenwriter's finest hour was the cult sci-fi horror film *Creature from the Black Lagoon* (1954). He had a talent for tapping into societal fears while entertaining people.

By the late 1950s, semidocumentary noir emerged as one distinct style. Scripts were often based on nonfiction sources. Scenes filmed in studios were mixed with those shot at real locations. Cities were characters. Cameras followed fictional investigators out on the city streets as they tried to get to the bottom of things. There were cops gone bad, wrongful convictions, and officials who went undercover to infiltrate the mob. Many of these stories, mixing entertainment with a social message, migrated from film to radio and then to television. Sometimes, the movement went the other way—from radio to television.[3] Whatever the medium, audiences had developed a taste for stories plucked from newspapers and investigators' records.

One such file belonged to Catherine Genovese, twenty-eight years old, of 82–70 Austin Street, Kew Gardens, New York City.[4] The redacted police reports released decades later were practically illegible. However, the focus of the investigation had soon shifted to those who witnessed the crime. This was what made this story—potentially—a documentary noir rather than a true crime story.

PERSONS OF INTEREST

Although numerous cracks appeared in the *New York Times* account of the murder of Genovese, it was not seriously challenged for decades.[5] Archival sleuthing revealed that there were not thirty-eight witnesses. The murder did not take place in full view of onlookers; no one could see the entire sequence of actions. Therefore, the event was not immediately identifiable as a serious crime. Further, there were two separate attacks, not three. One neighbor yelled, "Leave that girl alone!" While the *Times* reported that thirty-eight witnesses could have intervened during the attack, police records revealed that only two witnesses could feasibly have done so—the janitor in an apartment block across the street, and a gay man in the same building who, scared almost witless, took some time to reach a neighbor and call the police.

The initial *New York Times* report of the murder was buried deep in the newspaper. Sadly, the event was far from unusual; it was one of 636 murders in New York City that year. The brief article, published on March 14, 1964, opened with "A 28-year-old Queens woman was stabbed to death early yesterday morning outside her apartment in Kew Gardens. Neighbors who were awakened by her screams found the woman, Miss Catherine Genovese of 82–70 Austin Street, shortly after 3 A.M."[6] Initially, the crime warranted only a brief follow-up of what reporters termed the "police blotter" (a large book providing a chronological record of the events in a given precinct for the day). Police had spent the day searching for the murder weapon, interviewing witnesses, and checking the license plates of cars seen in the vicinity. At this stage, they had no clues.

Over the next two weeks, the murder of Genovese was reported by numerous other American newspapers. Predictably, New York tabloids tended to blame the victim. On March 14, the day after the rape and killing, the *New York Daily News* reported, "Knifed Barmaid Dies in Mystery."

Catherine Genovese did work in a bar; however, she was the manager. Her teenage marriage had been annulled. She "ran with a fast crowd" and lived in a bohemian neighborhood.[7] A black-and-white mug shot of Genovese, taken two years earlier when she was charged with a minor gambling offense, appeared to confirm this version. A police reconstruction made mention of neighbors who overheard her say, "I've been stabbed." The following day, detectives reported that "three or four witnesses" had seen a man attacking the victim.[8]

The *New York Herald Tribune* article "Help Cry Ignored, Girl Dies of Knifing" provided the first glimpse of that key image. "The neighbors had grandstand seats for the slaying of Kitty Genovese. And, yet, when the pretty diminutive twenty-eight-year-old brunette called for help, she called in vain," reported Robert Parrella the day after the murder.[9] Note the "grandstand seats"—as if people were watching a sporting event. Why did Parrella's version fail to capture the attention that the *New York Times* story soon would? In part, this was because it appeared on page 10 of a newspaper with considerably less prestige. More important, the *Herald Tribune* account lacked one telling detail. Then police commissioner Michael Murphy gave newly appointed *New York Times* city editor Abe Rosenthal a tip: there were thirty-eight witnesses to a murder down in Queens, and not one of them had contacted the police.[10] Rosenthal dispatched reporters to the neighborhood to interview witnesses and detectives working on the case. He personally line edited the resulting article, but apparently, no one did much fact-checking.

"For more than half an hour, 38 respectable, law-abiding citizens in Queens watched a killer stalk and stab a woman in three separate attacks in Kew Gardens," the *New York Times* lead story now claimed.[11] The case was baffling, said the veteran detective in charge of the investigation. "As we have reconstructed the crime, the assailant had three chances to kill the woman during a 35-minute period. . . . If we had been called when she was first attacked, she might not be dead now," he added. One witness told detectives, "I didn't want to get involved."

Much ink has since been spilled telling and retelling the Kitty Genovese story. Judging by the number of re-enactments and true crime stories it has inspired, the event makes detectives of us all. Long before the murder led to a program of social science research into (at least initially) public apathy, it was supposedly underpinned by those police reconstructions of the crime. Yet, the key details of the *New York Times* story owed more to imagination than facts. As psychologist Arthur Lurigio wrote, "The reporting was filled with inaccuracies." Each time the story was told, "the most resounding (and inaccurate) aspects were emphasized for dramatic effect."[12]

Reconstructions of crimes aim to flush out new evidence and develop plausible theories that can be tested. They involve gaining "explicit knowledge of the series of events that surround . . . a crime using deductive and inductive reasoning, physical evidence, scientific methods, and their inter-relationships."[13] As a popular character cautioned in an episode of the contemporary television series *CSI: Crime Scene Investigation*, "You don't crunch the evidence to fit a theory."[14] As far back as 1933, Luke May—author of the influential book *Scientific Murder Investigation*—considered that the true mark of an investigator was the ability to "work tirelessly, obtaining facts upon which to predicate theories, changing his initial theories as the facts developed."[15] Human testimony, in particular, should be treated with caution. Edward Heinrich, a legendary Berkeley-based consultant on criminal investigations and crime analysis, offered the analogy of a mosaic: "Every fact must be evaluated before it can fit into the pattern."[16]

The *New York Times* city editor Rosenthal took the story and ran with it. His follow-up article canvassed expert opinions on the puzzling behavior of Genovese's neighbors. Its subheading was practically an article itself: "Apathy Is Puzzle in Queens Killing: Behavioral Specialists Hard Put to Explain Witnesses' Failure to Call Police—Interpretations Vary—Some Say Tendency Not to Get Involved Is Typical Others Call It Uncommon."[17] Psychiatrists, psychologists, and sociologists all weighed in, but no real agreement was reached. Police stepped up their law-and-order campaign, encouraging people to report crime. Television was soon called out as part of the problem. "A confusion of fantasy with reality, fed by an endless stream of television violence, was in part responsible for the fact that 37 Queens residents could passively watch a murder take place," claimed one forensic psychiatrist.[18] Accumulated images damaged the brain. One wonders what he might have made of our current world of video streamed 24/7.

Thirty-Eight Witnesses, Rosenthal's nonfiction novella, was on the shelves of bookshops within months. In the early 1960s, Adolf Eichmann's trial for crimes against humanity was one of the world's first live television events. Rosenthal's account of onlookers who failed to intervene echoed—albeit on a much smaller scale—the Holocaust. In emotive language, the *New York Times* city editor held his fellow citizens to account for the murder of Kitty Genovese. Every one of those thirty-eight decent, middle-class people turned away when they heard a cry in the night, he wrote.[19]

A half-hour CBS radio program, "The Apathetic American," about "American fear and indifference in times of crisis," was broadcast in August 1964. It staged a re-creation of the murder, followed by a roundtable with social commentators.[20] Americans, it seemed, were not only apathetic but unengaged. A television documentary, *The Detached Americans*, drew on the Genovese parable to bookend an inquiry into civic values. The presenter appeared in the studio with a television set displaying a crime scene photograph—the chalked outline of a body on the pavement amid pools of blood. Thirty-eight witnesses watched the murder and then went to bed, he claimed. It was all in an evening's entertainment.

Warner Brothers soon took an option on Rosenthal's *Thirty-Eight Witnesses*.[21] As a nonfiction novella, the book was almost made for adaptation to the big screen. Nonfiction was in the news. Tom Wolfe claimed that his fellow feature writers at the *New York Herald Tribune*, experimenting with fictional techniques to produce livelier writing, invented New Journalism around this time. However, many other feature writers, including the *New Yorker's* John Hersey and Lillian Ross, had long been experimenting with the art of facts. Six months after the murder of Catherine Genovese, *Lonely Street* was being rushed into production. Leonard Kantor, whose credits included episodes of *M Squad* and *The*

Untouchables, which focused on elite police squads tackling organized crime and corruption, took over writing duties in mid-1964 and quickly produced two drafts. The title of the proposed film was changed to *Thirty-Eight Witnesses*.

The thinking woman's defense lawyer, Perry Mason, played by Raymond Burr, had a crack at the case in "The Case of the Silent Six," a 1965 episode of the popular long-running drama *Perry Mason*. (Presumably, the number of witnesses was reduced to six for budget reasons.) Mason defended a police officer falsely accused of killing a man who assaulted a young woman (figures 4.1 and 4.2.) Piecing together the evidence with his customary zeal, Mason confronted the real killer on the witness stand. "I'm guilty," the latter confessed. "But you're guiltier than I am!" He added, gazing around the courtroom, "either because you were too scared or too busy or you don't care."[22] His courtroom speech summed up the key reasons people made for not helping in the parable of the Good Samaritan—all of which were soon incorporated into social psychology's bystander experiments.

The Numbers

How did the story of one crime come to dominate bystander research? Social psychologists John Darley and Bibb Latane named four "crimes" that inspired their "Bystander Effect" experiments. All occurred in New York City within a year of the murder of Catherine Genovese.[23] The other incidents involved Olga Romero (assault), Andrew Mormille (murder), and Eleanor Bradley (who broke her leg while shopping). The shocking thing in each case was that so many people failed to help.

I went looking for more information. The sources appeared to be newspaper accounts. No record of the incident involving Bradley could be located. It was unlikely that such a minor accident would have made the news. Perhaps, I speculated, the psychologists heard about her ordeal from a friend or colleague? I soon moved on to the case of Olga Romero. "Rape Victim's Screams Draw 40, but No One Acts," read the headline for Thomas Buckley's story in the *New York Times* less than a month after the murder of Genovese.[24] Eighteen-year-old switchboard operator Olga Romero was violently assaulted by a traveling salesman in a deserted office building. Only when the young woman managed to escape and reached the ground floor entrance, her attacker still in pursuit, did others became aware of her plight. According to court statements, a naked and bleeding Romero screamed, "Help me, help me, I've been raped." People gathered outside the building. "The crowd of onlookers . . . stood silent and immobile, heedless to the girl's pleas," reported Buckley.[25] Two police officers on their way to work came to her aid. Patrolman Brown and his partner pushed through the crowd to save the young woman. They arrested the man she identified as her attacker and called the station for backup.

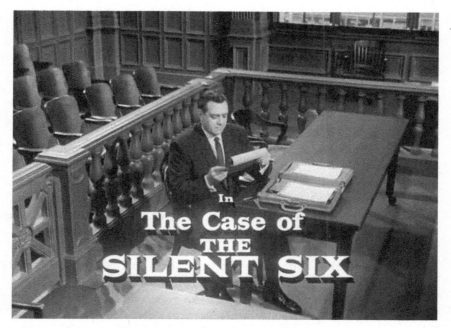

Figure 4.1. *Perry Mason*, "The Case of the Silent Six," 1965.

Figure 4.2. *Perry Mason*, "The Case of the Silent Six," 1965.

"Forty people could have helped that girl yesterday but none of the jerks helped her," Brown said in court.[26] Because he and his partner did not take any witness statements, there was no corroboration of the estimated crowd numbers. Buckley visited the crime scene before filing his *New York Times* story, but "no one could be found yesterday who had seen the attack or had heard the young woman's screams." There existed chilling echoes of the rape and murder of Genovese. This time, however, readers were confronted with an image of a faceless crowd. It could almost have been a zombie movie.

The brutal stabbing of Andrew Mormille as he returned home from an outing to Coney Island with his girlfriend was a media sensation. Police reported that the murder occurred in front of approximately ten passengers seated in the same train carriage. Yet, according to the press, no one went to Mormille's aid or would help police identify his killers.[27] Detectives rode the subway for days afterward with a sketch of the suspect, a composite based on witnesses' descriptions. "We are in desperate need of assistance," said the detective in charge. "How can we solve the crime if the people who saw it won't come forward?"[28] Tabloids ran graphic crime scene shots of the teenager's body slumped on the floor of an empty train carriage in a pool of blood.[29] However, contrary to the headlines, some people did help the police—three teenage girls, accompanied by their mothers, eventually came forward. The alleged killer had harassed them before knifing Mormille. They had been too terrified to speak.

These four events all resonated with concerns about the dangers of living in the big city. People's failure to intervene was attributed to everything from apathy and the lack of connection between people in urban environments to the impact of watching too much television (much like contemporary concerns about people spending too much time in front of screens). Perpetrators were apprehended relatively quickly. Inevitably, court cases focused on establishing the case for prosecution rather than the failure of multiple eyewitnesses to offer help. In the court of public opinion, however, the case against the groups of onlookers who failed to intervene was still to be prosecuted.

Due to the practical and ethical difficulties of staging violence, psychologists' first experiments were based on minor incidents and improvised primarily in universities. They included a simulated fit, a woman falling, and a smoke-filled room. The "simulated fit" scenario was intended to replicate the dynamics of the Genovese murder by isolating participants. Male and female students were placed individually in a room equipped with headphones and a microphone and asked to listen for instructions. They soon overheard a victim crying for help. In the "fallen woman" scenario, subjects were invited to participate in a survey of puzzle preferences. They were provided with a variety of materials to evaluate while the experimenter left to work nearby. Participants soon heard a loud crash followed by a woman's scream, "Oh my god, my foot, I . . . I can't move it. . . . I can't get this thing off me." Last, students recruited as volunteers were asked to report to a room and fill in a survey. While they were waiting, smoke began to trickle under the door. This was intended to simulate an ambiguous but potentially dangerous situation.

Accepting an award for their initial research in 1969, Darley and Latane summarized their depressing findings. There was a clear explanation for the apathy of those who saw Genovese murdered. It may sound counterintuitive, but the likelihood of any one person acting as a Good Samaritan in an emergency decreased as the number of witnesses increased. Most people were cowards, ready to pass the buck and convince themselves that someone else could take care of an emergency. "It was considered embarrassing to look overly concerned, to seem flustered, to lose your cool your public"[30]—we were (mostly) Bad Samaritans.

Good Samaritans

For seven and a half minutes in 1968, hundreds of New York City subway passengers formed a captive audience as a man struggled to his feet and collapsed. In repeated scenarios, a concerned fellow passenger was usually kneeling at his side within seventy seconds, reported Irving, Jane Piliavin, and Judith Rodin. By staging emergency scenarios on the subway, they hoped to achieve greater realism than was possible in a university laboratory. Four different men—three white and one black—were cast in the victim role. During some trials, the victim smelled of alcohol and appeared to be drunk. In others, he used a cane and appeared blind. Overwhelmingly, the latter received help from passengers, and the victim who seemed drunk was assisted far less often. The researchers noted that people were more likely to empathize with someone of their own race and ethnicity. They did not find that the presence of greater numbers of people prevented people from helping in emergencies[31]—we were (mostly) Good Samaritans.

The Good Samaritan experiments received considerably less press attention than the Bad Samaritan experiments. Some journalists even described them as "phony dramas."[32] The same criticism was not made of the incidents staged by Darley and Latane, although both research teams devised short scenarios and staged them with nonprofessional actors (usually student volunteers). Whether they featured Good or Bad Samaritans, none of the scenarios devised for bystander research captured the collective imagination outside classrooms and lecture theaters. Their dramatic stakes were low—the simulations lacked not only vivid imagery but also the potential for dramatic action and characterization. The Piliavin and Rodin subway experiments do not appear to have been filmed. The Darley and Latane experiments have proved to be best suited to restaging for educational documentaries or current affairs programs in which commentators could discuss their findings.

LEADS NOT FOLLOWED

When he first arrived in New York City to take up a new appointment, Stanley Milgram found the city a nightmare. Leaving Grand Central, he was caught up in pushing, shoving crowds: "Why were people so rushed? Even drunks on the streets were passed without a glance. People didn't seem to care about each other at all."[33] Milgram was one of the first social psychologists to seek an explanation for the behavior of the alleged thirty-eight witnesses in the Genovese murder. "We are all certain that we could have done better," Milgram and sociologist Paul Hollander wrote in a 1964 article for the *Nation*. There were real dangers in becoming involved in violent situations, and it was foolish to ignore them. The anger toward the residents of Kew Gardens was such that one senator read the *New York Times* article aloud to Congress so that it could become part of the official record. But where was that same senator when the murder of black people occurred in his home state in front of white onlookers who did not protest? Directing their attention back to the Genovese murder, Milgram and Hollander speculated that each person might have believed that someone else was taking action. Why did the onlookers not band together, run out into the street, and tackle the assailant? Apart from issues of time and organization, they were ill-equipped to do so. Vilifying ordinary citizens was not the answer. This was Milgram at his best—the streetwise psychologist tuned in to the world around him.

In the summer of 1960, Milgram and some friends traveled out of New York City, improvising street theater scenes. Stopping at restaurants and gas stations along a major route, they staged scenes of conflict. Their improvisations featured an irate woman who discovers her husband has been unfaithful. Despite scenes of heightened emotion, onlookers avoided involvement even when the husband was physically aggressive toward his wife. Returning to Harvard, Milgram wrote up a set of experiments in which subjects would overhear such an argument. At a predetermined cue, the woman would cry out for help. Who, if anyone, would intervene? And at what point? Milgram's proposed studies were called the "social intrusion" experiments. Not long afterward, the twenty-something psychologist was appointed to his first ongoing academic position at Yale University. Working with students, Milgram progressed the idea via an experiment about a woman abused in a laundromat by a drunk.[34] (The "Obedience to Authority" experiments were also initially workshopped with students.) As it turned out, the obedience work took off. Milgram put the "social intrusion" experiments aside, and the moment to return to them never quite arrived.

What might Milgram's unstaged bystander experiments have looked and sounded like? It is safe to say that they would have been far more dramatic than either the Good Samaritan or the Bad Samaritan experiments. From the beginning, Milgram understood that the gender of people in conflict was a critical factor in whether onlookers intervened to help. The article in the *Nation* suggested he was also aware that the race of those requiring help was significant. Alone among his generation of social psychologists, Milgram was able to take observations from life and give them dramatic expression—sketching preliminary thoughts, workshopping scenarios with student or social actors, feeding insights back into the experimental design. His dramatic experiments may have made headlines (and not always for good reasons), but they were never simply torn from the headlines.

Writing in *Life* magazine not long after the Genovese rape and murder story broke, journalist and editor Loudon Wainwright described the experiments thus: "For the most part, the witnesses, crouching in darkened windows like watchers of a *Late Show*, looked on until the play had passed from their view."[35] The event itself was already drama. It is hardly surprising that the thirty-eight witnesses who watched a woman being murdered—as if they were viewing late-night television—overshadowed the small-scale drama of psychologists' experiments.

Research into the bystander effect continued for decades. According to Jane Piliavin—summarizing the evolution of research on altruism and helping—by the 1980s, it was clear that the numbers were not the only factor. Rather, the combined efforts of many researchers in the social sciences demonstrated that some people help under some circumstances in some emergencies. Collectively, we were Not-So-Bad Samaritans. Unfortunately, this more nuanced explanation was not the stuff of headlines.

Witness to a Killing

Eventually, I located the screenplay for *Lonely Street* by Harry Essex in the University of Southern California Warner Brothers Archive in Los Angeles. One alternative title was *38 Witnesses*. Although the materials were deposited in the archive donated by Warner Brothers to the University of Southern California, the files stayed firmly shut. (Unless you are on the West Coast of the United States, copying and digitization are not permitted.) The latest title was revealing—*Witness to a Killing*—a noir title if ever I have heard one.

Not long after purchasing the rights to Essex's story, Warner Brothers signed on William Conrad as producer and director. Conrad was a Hollywood heavyweight, a larger-than-life figure who began his career playing thugs and heavies. He was also the voice of hundreds of crime stories for film, radio, and television. In 1963, Conrad began a long stint as narrator on the hugely popular series *The Fugitive*. Every episode began the same way. Out of the darkness, the lights of a train rush toward us. Inside the train, a man in a suit is guarded by a detective; an innocent man, he has been convicted of murder and is headed for death row. Suddenly, all is chaos. The train comes off the rails, and the prisoner slips away. As in its big-screen noir counterparts, *The Fugitive*'s narration combines exposition with insights into characters' mental states. "Walk neither too fast nor too slow, beware the eyes of strangers, keep moving," William Conrad intones as the eponymous fugitive takes his first steps under an assumed identity.[36] Oddly, those particular lines could serve double duty for a woman walking alone at night—a woman like Catherine Genovese. Keep moving. Do not meet anyone's eyes. Be ready to break into a sprint.

In her insightful book, *The Stubborn Particulars of Social Psychology*, Frances Cherry highlights that the initial bystander experiments revealed at least as much about the preoccupations of American social science in the 1960s as they did about the behavior of bystanders. That era's research imperative was to generate broad theories about human behavior to be tested under laboratory conditions. In the process, important details were erased, including gender, race, sexuality, class, and age. Cherry proposed reinserting some of those details in the picture. One start, she suggested, might be shifting the focus from "there was an emergency, and no one intervened to help" to "violence was directed at yet another woman by a man and no one intervened to help."[37]

The fortieth anniversary of Genovese's rape and murder saw the story in the news once again. In 2004, prompted by research by Kew Gardens resident Jo De May, the *New York Times* finally admitted that there were gaps in its story about the thirty-eight witnesses.[38] De May, a maritime lawyer, pored over the legal documentation, including trial transcripts. Conducting his own investigation, he even ran up and down the stairs of Genovese's building with a stopwatch. He concluded that the vast majority of witnesses did not see any part of the attack— what people saw or heard was fleeting and vague. Social psychologist Mark Levine attributed the lack of attention to situations in which groups of people *do* help to the parable of the thirty-eight witnesses: "Due to the power [of the Genovese story] we rarely . . . look at situations where the power of the collective can actually enhance intervention."[39]

THE WITNESS

"I want you to squeeze the neighborhood dry. Make the people talk," a detective told his colleagues in *Death Scream* (1975), a made-for-television thriller based on the Genovese murder.[40] The telemovie opened with the familiar re-creation of a young woman arriving home late at night and screaming as she is savagely attacked. People watched from their flats but did not help. The murder of Genovese has been re-enacted repeatedly, but never so powerfully as in the closing moments of the feature documentary *The Witness* (2016).[41]

The film had its genesis in a scripted film about Kitty Genovese written by director James Solomon for Home Box Office. However, the feature drama did not come to fruition, and Solomon returned to other writing projects. In 2004, the fortieth anniversary of the murder, he read the *New York Times* article that had raised questions about the accuracy of the newspaper's account of the thirty-eight witnesses. The director proposed to Bill Genovese—Catherine Genovese's younger brother, whom he had met on the research trail—that they document their search on camera.

Bill Genovese was sixteen years old when his sister was raped and murdered. After spending many years not wanting to know what happened that night, he came to the realization that "not knowing was worse than knowing." He wanted to create a sense of his sister as a person, not as a victim or as collateral damage to the bystander effect. Solomon and his collaborators spent eleven years documenting Bill Genovese's relentless quest to track down everyone he could to learn more about what had happened to his sister. Their interview subjects included neighbors, detectives, and journalists—the latter group in the attempt to explain how the story became so huge. It is Bill Genovese who eventually "makes the people talk." No potential witness escapes his interrogation. He discovered, among other things, that crime reporters at the time were highly skeptical of the *New York Times* claim regarding the thirty-eight witnesses—it was simply inconsistent with police reports. However, they did not come forward to contest the story.

The murder of his much-loved older sister and the apparent passivity of the onlookers shaped Bill Genovese's life. He attributed his decision to enlist in the U.S. Marine Corps and fight in the Vietnam War to the events of March 13, 1964. Growing up, he resolved always to be an actor in history rather than a bystander. Bill Genovese was badly wounded in Vietnam and became paraplegic. The difference between himself and Kitty, he said in one of the film's closing scenes, is that colleagues risked their lives to rescue him—he was not left to die alone. Crucially, he ultimately discovered that his sister was not left to do so either. A female neighbor who was a close friend of Catherine Genovese went to investigate the scene, called the police, and stayed with Catherine until the police arrived.

The Witness is skillfully shot, edited, and directed. Solomon, who had extensive story editing and writing credits on legal dramas, put his deep knowledge of the genre to good use. As he conducts his investigation, Bill Genovese pins up photographs of witnesses on the wall. Line-drawn animation sequences function as the "crazy wall" of the police procedural, allowing us to review key evidence (figure 4.3). Documentary theorist Bill Nichols has proposed that the use of animation in documentaries is inherently reflexive. It can invite viewers to "question the assumption that a documentary must support its proposals or perspective with historically authentic footage."[42] In this case, the line drawings' provisional nature draws attention to our incomplete knowledge of the event.

The film ends with Bill Genovese witnessing an actress re-create the last minutes of his sister's life on the street at night outside her former apartment. Filmed from multiple perspectives, the scene functions as crime scene reconstruction writ large. It is the culmination of an exhaustive investigation to which we—the audience—have been privy. Will it flush out new evidence? As the actress runs along the street at night, screaming in terror, Bill Genovese forces himself

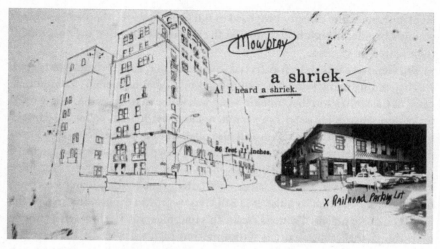

Figure 4.3. *The Witness*, FilmRise, 2015.

to watch. *The Witness* does not offer the tidy resolution of true crime stories. Instead, the filmmakers encourage us to review the evidence for ourselves. The research documents obtained by the filmmakers' investigators are included in the "special features" customarily provided on DVDs. Here, James Solomon and Bill Genovese generously hand over their case notes to the audience.

BREAKING THE STORY

Journalists aim to break the story—to obtain a scoop and be the first to tell a story, such as one about thirty-eight witnesses to a murder. Essayist and nonfiction writer Rebecca Solnit, who began her career in journalism, has said that those responsibilities go much further. It is not enough to simply report the story on the surface—the contained story, the one that happened yesterday. Rather, public storytellers are duty bound "to see and make visible and sometimes break open or break apart the ambient stories, the stories that are already written, and to understand the relationship between the two."[43] News is often said to be the first draft of history. Sometimes, those early drafts are wrong.

Stefani Tani, my favorite writer on detective narratives, devised a category he called anti–detective stories.[44] The genre stresses social criticism, solutions in which justice does not always prevail, and the inability of the investigator to remain detached. The investigator risks everything to find a solution. Finally, they stop following up new leads and admit the mystery. Even if the investigator has not found the solution, they have understood something about their own quest. This, I think, is true of Bill Genovese at the end of *The Witness*. The myth associated with his sister has been unraveled. Inevitably, there is still more to discover, but he calls it quits. Perhaps we should call it quits on reenacting the rape and murder of Catherine Genovese?

The trail connected to Catherine Genovese is littered with untold stories. So far, the story has not been adapted successfully for cinema. However, in 2017, independent film powerhouse Killer Films announced that David Russell would direct a drama adaptation of Solomon's *The Witness*. The project is still in development. Will watching a Hollywood actor as Bill Genovese finally change the story and shift public perceptions about the bystander effect?

Social scientists continue to seek an understanding of how groups of onlookers behave in public emergencies. One strand of contemporary research focuses on the analysis of CCTV footage sourced from publicly funded surveillance centers: most notably, the work of United Kingdom–based psychologist Mark Levine and sociologist Charlotte Bloch in Denmark. New insights continue to emerge. Fundamentally, the work of Levine, Bloch, and their collaborators focuses on the ways bystanders successfully intervene to help in violent emergencies.[45] Their stories are sourced from the streets—in the form of redacted CCTV footage or smartphone video filmed by those who witness racist incidents on public transport. While these audiovisual records are often partial and incomplete, they provide evidence of real-life scenarios.

Parables—scientific or otherwise—are teaching stories. They are not best equipped to deal with complexity and nuance. Instead, they aim to cut through the static to explore important moral dilemmas. A story shifts during each retelling. The parable of Catherine Genovese is built on misinformation. As Rebecca Solnit said, people talk about stories as if they were all wonderful. However, stories—like Samaritans—can be good or bad.

On the eve of his assassination in 1968, civil rights activist Dr. Martin Luther King recounted the Good Samaritan parable to a large gathering of low-paid workers on strike. King highlighted that it was a man of another race who finally helped the stranger robbed and beaten on the road to Jericho. Why did the other passersby not help? Perhaps they were frightened? Perhaps they were in a hurry, on their way to an important meeting? The man who helped the traveler in need fundamentally reframed the question, said King. He did not ask, "What will happen *to me* if I help this man? Instead, he asked, what will happen *to him* if I don't help?"

According to Levine and Bloch, their respective analyses of hundreds of violent incidents culled from surveillance footage sourced from the United Kingdom, Denmark, and South Africa have revealed that most people help. Their research is ongoing. The parable of Genovese remains a factor that complicates the search for new insights. New work in social psychology focuses not on the apathetic bystander but rather on the "caring collective." John Drury and colleagues have long explored the processes involved in the collective resilience typically displayed in public emergencies.[46] More broadly, the social sciences are paying renewed attention to qualities such as empathy and kindness.[47] But, as every filmmaker, storyteller, or actor knows, it is much more fun to tell the story of the bad guys than the good guys.

To date, the real untold stories are not those languishing in the archives of film studios. They are the stories of strangers who cooperate to intervene in public crises. Perhaps we are (mostly) Good Samaritans? At the very least, we are Not-So-Bad Samaritans.

CHAPTER 5

Doing Time

On a quiet Sunday morning in August 1971 in Palo Alto, California, police cars sweep through town, picking up college students. A mass arrest of people wanted for robbery is taking place. Now, as their concerned neighbors and families look on, those assigned the role of prisoners are arrested, strip-searched, and handcuffed. Sirens wailing, real-life cops blindfold them and drive them to prison for processing, albeit a purpose-built prison in the basement of Stanford University's psychology building. The selected students had answered an advertisement seeking volunteers. It read, "Male college students needed for psychological study of prison life. $15 per day for 1–2 weeks beginning August 14th. For further information and application, come to Room 248, Jordan Hall, Stanford University."[1]

It is a scorching summer's day, one year earlier. In the desert, 62.1 miles (100 kilometers) from Los Angeles, groups of young people stagger across harsh terrain. Their aim is to reach an American flag fluttering in the wind. Cops, their batons and handcuffs at the ready, are in hot pursuit. Clouds of dust make it difficult to see exactly what is going on. Is it a training exercise? A social experiment? In fact, all the participants are nonprofessional actors. These scenes are from Peter Watkins's independent feature *Punishment Park* (1971), shot on location in California.[2] They feature in the trailer for the film, released not long before Philip Zimbardo ran his "Stanford Prison Experiment."

These two dramas, staged for the camera in California in the early 1970s, had some similarities. Both the "Stanford Prison Experiment" and *Punishment Park* featured nonprofessional actors playing members of opposing tribes and drew, in part, on improvisation. Both aimed to contribute to social change. But their affinities end there. The "Stanford Prison Experiment," in which Zimbardo cast himself as the prison's superintendent—and abandoned any sense of oversight—claimed the status of scientific experiment. *Punishment Park*, an independent film by British filmmaker Peter Watkins, aimed to provoke public debate by staging scenarios involving political and social conflict. Its experimentation was primarily artistic. Arguably, however, the methods of radical film and theater makers of the 1960s and 1970s—such as Peter Watkins, Augusto Boal, and the Living Theatre—helped Zimbardo bring his social psychology story to broad audiences.

When it comes to the "Stanford Prison Experiment," my question is: How does it stack up against alternative theater and film productions of the 1960s and 1970s that took prisons as their subject? I am thinking specifically about playwright Kenneth Brown's *The Brig* (1963), Jonas Mekas's documentary of the Living Theatre production of *The Brig* (1963), and Peter Watkins's *Punishment Park* (1971).

The "Stanford Prison Experiment," still the best-known psychology experiment of our era, has shadowed me throughout my adult life. Did I really first hear about it as a young residential care worker? Or was it as an arts student enrolled in a large introductory psychology course (Psych. 101, or "Rats and Stats" as it was better known) at Adelaide University in the middle to late 1970s? As we railed against an outdated curriculum—relevance was everything, in our book—contemporary experiments addressing challenging questions about social behavior were especially welcome. The "Stanford Prison Experiment" continued to stalk me through a series of community activist, youth worker, and film culture worker jobs over the next decade, and my subsequent career as an independent filmmaker and academic. Wherever I was, talk of the "Stanford Prison Experiment" never seemed far away. Its official narrative is this—randomly assigned a role such as that of guard or prisoner, our behavior is true to type. We will most likely brutalize others or withdraw and become victims. Never convinced by its findings, I have actively followed news of the experiment for decades.

Millions of words have been written and spoken about the "Stanford Prison Experiment." Its instigator and others have made many claims. It is an experiment, a simulation, a role play, a demonstration, and evidence. As the decades have slipped by, the claims about the experiment as drama have grown dramatically. It is a Greek drama on an epic scale. It is like a Hollywood movie. It is a story of good and evil. Whatever it is, it is slippery—hard to bring into clear focus. My detective father's investigative motto, "Stick to the facts," will probably not help me this time. Whose facts? There has been evidence enough to sink the "Stanford Prison Experiment" for decades. Yet it continues to crowd fresh insights about social behavior out of the picture, leaving them languishing in the dark. Why? I bring my own line of inquiry back to the center. It has two foci: story and social drama.

STORY

Opening my laptop, I searched for the official website of the "Stanford Prison Experiment."[3] The information, or at least some of it, is found easily enough. The Google search engine and its algorithms took a little over a second to return

4,240,000 results. None of the critiques made of the experiment appeared near the top of the list. Those places were, of course, reserved for those who paid for the privilege. It was difficult to differentiate between the "Stanford Prison Experiment," staged in 1971, and the Hollywood film *The Stanford Prison Experiment*, produced in 2015.[4] The official website for the experiment, now barely distinguishable from that of the movie, presents Zimbardo's account as "The Story: An Overview of the Experiment."

The experiment, if this is what it was, began on August 14, 1971. Originally planned to run for two weeks, it was shut down nine days ahead of schedule when Christina Maslach, recently awarded her doctorate in psychology, became concerned about the abuse of prisoners she was observing. Maslach persuaded Zimbardo, whom she was soon to marry, to end the experiment. How did news of the "Stanford Prison Experiment" first break? Stories appeared the day after Zimbardo abandoned his experiment, with headlines such as "Prison Experiment Just Too Realistic" and "Prison Test Halted—Too Brutal."[5]

The Stanford professor had selected the twelve guards and their prisoners from more than seventy applicants. Anyone whose preliminary personality tests suggested they might be too sadistic was excluded. The simulation was set up in three windowless and barred rooms in the basement of the Stanford psychology department. It was stopped when one-third of the guards became brutal and tyrannical, and three prisoners suffered breakdowns. "It was no longer a simulation of a prison," Zimbardo said.[6] A whole new level of reality had been created. His experiment was the real deal.

Accompanying black-and-white stills appeared to underscore Zimbardo's point. (Two prisoners dressed in uniforms resembling hospital gowns gaze out from behind the bars of their cell. His back to the camera, a guard watches them. All three men sport the long hair favored by many students of the era (figure 5.1). A guard, wearing mirrored sunglasses and holding a baton, poses by a sign reading "Stanford County Prison." (This guard came to be known as "John Wayne" after the tough guy film actor.) In this picture, he appears more threatening (figure 5.2). Neither image seems particularly realistic. The costumes and hairstyles do not look like they would conform to any jail's uniform regulations. The prisoners do not seem particularly troubled; rather, any sense of conflict is inferred by the juxtaposition of the two images and the behavior reported by the experimenter.

Delving into the newspaper archives, I found several articles that appeared a month or so earlier, praising ex-prisoner Carlo Prescott's Stanford seminar "The Psychology of Being Imprisoned."[7] Prescott, who "knew what it was to do time," had served sixteen years in prison—most recently for armed robbery. The course he was teaching, organized by Zimbardo, was funded via a grant from the National Institute of Mental Health. To avoid political battles within the university, Zimbardo registered himself as the convenor. In fact, he sat in while Prescott

Figure 5.1. "Stanford Prison Experiment," 1971. Photographer: Chuck Painter. Special Collections and University Archives, Stanford University.

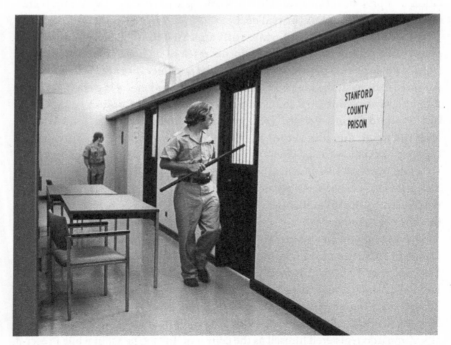

Figure 5.2. "Stanford Prison Experiment," 1971. Photographer: Chuck Painter. Special Collections and University Archives, Stanford University.

gave all the lectures and set and graded assignments. It was deemed important that students learn criminal psychology from someone who had firsthand
experience of penal institutions. Only one participant had withdrawn after
finding the experience "a bit intense." By all accounts, Prescott was a forceful and
engaging presence on campus. Two hours after one particular class had finished, a
group of students remained, debating the ideas presented. Their teacher was
pushing the idea that society was a whole lot of prisons, said one. They were
learning about the "prisons of the mind."

Zimbardo quickly followed up his "Stanford Prison Experiment" press release
with more media interviews. The experiment had only just come to a dramatic
halt. There were no opportunities for any of the participants to step out of their
roles and reflect. Zimbardo was in no position to help, since he had assigned himself the leading role. The experimenter acknowledged that the participants
became trapped in their roles. In his view, though, this only added to the credibility of his experiment. The researchers had created a mock prison in which
people were suffering. The prisoners withdrew psychologically while several of
their jailers behaved sadistically. Authority figures relished their power. The les-
sons? First, prison reform was needed to stop the psychological brutalization of
both guards and prisoners. Second, people should be aware of the power of the
situation over their individual behavior. We all walk around under the illusion
that we have more control of situations than we actually possess. Any of us are
capable of behaving like the prisoners or guards in the Stanford role play.

In the slide-tape show in which Zimbardo initially reported his findings, a
surprising number of images were devoted to the recent riots at the Attica Prison.
Confrontation. Prison layout. Dead bodies on the floor of prison cells. Newspaper headlines. These graphic black-and-white images were intercut with (mostly)
color slides of the Stanford simulation: high-contrast images of the fictional student prisoners being picked up by the police, sitting in cells, or performing the
tasks requested by their nominal guards.

The classic postwar social psychology experiments were conducted in
purpose-built settings—like Milgram's psychology laboratory or Zimbardo's
prison—or public locations. The latter included institutions, streets, buses, or
trains. Whatever the setting, though, experimenters consciously linked their
studies to real-world events. The Holocaust. Kitty Genovese's rape and murder
in 1964. In this case, the Attica Prison riot. Zimbardo's experiment seemed to
provide the story behind the headlines.

From within psychology and the social sciences, Zimbardo's simulation was
criticized from its inception. The debate about ethics that it generated led the
American Psychological Association to tighten its guidelines regarding participants. Leon Festinger, responsible for his field's influential cognitive dissonance experiments, wrote that "one can improvise a goal and have subjects
volunteer . . . One can report some interesting and newsworthy reactions from

Figure 5.3. Prisoners, *The Experiment*, BBC Television, 2002.

those individuals."[8] However, this was not an experiment. No hypothesis had been identified in advance, no variables had been identified and tested, and no new knowledge was produced.

In 2002, British psychologists Alex Haslam and Steve Reicher devised and ran their own prison experiment in collaboration with the BBC.[9] Simultaneously, broadcasters were turning their attention to "social experiment" television as a means of reinvigorating nonfiction and history programming. As British Film Institute television curator Lisa Kerrigan has noted, "Social experiments have proven to be extremely useful to program makers. Though constructing situations is not the traditional preserve of documentaries, the opportunities afforded by placing participants in unusual scenarios can provide genuine revelations."[10]

In this case, the researchers aimed to explore the social and psychological consequences of placing people in groups possessing unequal power (figure 5.3). The psychologists asked: What happens when people variously accept or challenge inequality?[11] Haslam and Reicher were clear that their own study was not a straightforward reprise of Zimbardo's "Stanford Prison Experiment." Like Zimbardo, they set up a prisonlike environment with guards and prisoners. Unlike Zimbardo, however, they did not involve themselves directly in the running of the mock prison. "On the one hand, as experimenters we were careful not to take a leadership role and tell the guards how they should behave," they wrote. "On the other hand, we designed a series of interventions, based on the predictions of social identity theory, to investigate the conditions under which prisoners would either adapt to or challenge the inequalities of the prison system."[12] An ethics panel was also appointed.

The BBC's advertisement "Do you really know yourself?" called for volunteers who would take part in a "university-backed social science experiment to be shown on TV." Potential participants were warned that they would be exposed to "exercise, tasks, hardship, hunger, solitude and anger." No payment was offered, and there was no suggestion that participation would lead to fame. Instead, the producers from the BBC's factual programs department suggested that participation "might change the way you think."[13] In total, 322 people responded. They were asked to undertake three stages of screening: psychometric tests, a telephone interview, and a full clinical interview with independent clinical psychologists. The aim was to reject anyone who might be vulnerable to arrive at a selection of well-adjusted men.[14] However, one aspect of the experiment that was not updated was the exclusion of women. The four-part series was filmed on a prison set constructed at Elstree Studios in Hertfordshire.

Haslam and Reicher have described *The Experiment* as "an experiment filmed rather than a fictional drama."[15] They found no evidence of guards or prisoners blindly following roles. Alex Holmes, one of the executive producers and creative director, was the spokesperson for the BBC during the production and edit. He, too, noted that "the guards did not want to adopt their roles. They felt uncomfortable, which made them ineffective, whereas the prisoners were a more unified group."[16] Filming finished slightly early on the advice of ethics advisers and social psychologists. Participants, particularly those in the prisoner roles, were observed to be experiencing high levels of stress.

One of the difficulties posed by psychology experiments such as the "Obedience to Authority" studies and the "Stanford Prison Experiment" is that their ethics are subject to considerable controversy. This makes it extremely difficult for experimenters to restage such experiments to build on or challenge their findings. Attempts that meet ethical protocols almost inevitably dial down the drama. The social experiment television format creates both opportunities and challenges. Like many narratives claiming the authority of science, it can result in a closed rather than open text—that is, a book or program that leads people to one interpretation rather than a multiplicity of interpretations. *The Experiment* may be seen as a significant attempt by television program makers and social psychologists to revisit a classic experiment in an ethical and engaging manner. It brings cutting-edge social science to broad audiences, posing questions about the nature of both tyranny and rebellion. It has generated a wealth of insights and research into the processes of social change. (I should note here that it was Haslam and Reicher's publications on the social psychology of resistance that later led me to approach them to collaborate on a very different film revisiting Stanley Milgram's "Obedience to Authority.")

More recently, social scientist and filmmaker Thibault Le Texier became interested in the "Stanford Prison Experiment" when he discovered that it had been filmed with hidden cameras.[17] Le Texier, based in France, visited the Stanford University and other archives in the United States, intending to make a documentary based on the original tapes. Initially, he had no reason to doubt the official narrative. As he delved into the archival materials, however, he was shocked by the discrepancies between Zimbardo's account and the documentation. Zimbardo claimed that the guards were given no specific instructions or training, that they made up their own set of rules and were free (within limits) to do whatever they thought necessary to maintain order in the prison. Le Texier abandoned his proposed film, deciding that a book would better suit his purposes by allowing him to provide details of his archival sources. Consequently, he wrote *Histoire d'un mensonge (History of a Lie)*.[18]

The story uncovered by Le Texier goes like this. Zimbardo's experiment was based on a prison simulation run by students in a Stanford University "Social Psychology in Action" seminar run several months earlier. A small group of students worked together on a project about how prisoners were affected by being held in jails. While conducting research, they met the former prisoner Carlo Prescott. The students ran their prison simulation in the Toyon Hall dormitory at Stanford over one weekend with Prescott as their adviser. The simulation involved six guards and six prisoners. An undergraduate played the role of the tyrannical warden. A schedule and list of prison regulations structured their simulation. The strict daily schedule included prisoner counts and exercises. Key rules included the following:

10. Prisoners must address each other by number only. Inquiry into real name is forbidden.
11. Prisoners must always address the male guards as "Mr. Correctional Officer" and the female guards as "Miss Correctional Officer." [Unlike the "Stanford Prison Experiment," the student-run prison simulation involved both male and female prisoners and guards.] Prisoners must address the Warden as "Mister/Chief Correctional Officer."
13. Prisoners must obey all orders issued by guards at all times.[19]

The students reported that, at first, the prisoners tried to assert their individuality, but soon they obeyed the guards. The one exception was a female prisoner who resisted until the end. Feelings ran high. According to Le Texier, Zimbardo aimed to re-create the same outcome. The "Stanford Prison Experiment" used many of the same procedures as the student simulation: participants were formally arrested, shackled, stripped, made to wear a uniform, and identified only by a number when they arrived at the mock prison. A comparison of the daily schedule and regulations shows that the "Stanford Prison Experiment" script was almost identical to that of the student-led simulation run three months earlier. Moreover, three students who ran that simulation participated in the "Stanford Prison Experiment." Reporting directly to Zimbardo, who cast himself as superintendent, they were given the task of eliciting the desired behavior. Le Texier delved into the archival evidence: documents, photographs, audiotapes, and videotapes. Audiotapes clearly revealed the guards being coached.[20] Despite the millions of words floating around about the "Stanford Prison Experiment," no one had previously produced this evidence.

Following the link provided by Le Texier, I listened to the archival recording and watched the gray sound display turn orange as that critical one minute and eleven seconds played back.[21] We hear David Jaffe, one of the students who ran the Toyon Hall simulation and was the warden in Zimbardo's experiment. Jaffe speaks softly as he directs a reluctant guard:

> JAFFE: Generally, you've been kind of in the background. Part of that is my fault because I've gone along with when you wanted to sit outside while they were doing the count. Because the guards have to know that every guard is going to be what we call a tough guard. And so far——
>
> GUARD: I'm not too tough.
>
> WARDEN: Well, you have to try and get it in you.
>
> GUARD: Well, I don't know about that.
>
> WARDEN: See, the thing is, what I mean by tough is that you have to be firm and you have to be in the action and that sort of thing. It's really important for the workings of the experiment because whether or not we can make this thing seem like a prison, which is the aim of the thing, depends largely on the guard's behavior.

This evidence blew Zimbardo's story right out of the water. Stanford Prison was a demonstration, not an experiment.

Once again, an alternative story did not stick. To the best of his knowledge, Le Texier was the first person to explore the "Stanford Prison Experiment" archive systematically. (It is unclear when the recordings became available for independent scrutiny—most likely around 2017.) He was surprised that his new evidence did not attract more media attention. One commentator dismissed the new evidence and analysis. The "Stanford Prison Experiment" was now a story bigger than science. Writing for the *New York Times* about the field's crisis, science journalist Benedict Carey claimed that "many famous studies of human behavior cannot be reproduced. Even so, they reveal aspects of our inner life that feel true."[22] Feel true? Can that be right?

Stories have their own life cycles. New stories most often emerge from the margins or the edges. I refer back to the writer and activist Rebecca Solnit on the notion of "breaking the story." Reporters often use this phrase to refer to obtaining a scoop or being the first person to tell a particular story. For Solnit, breaking the story involves going further than simply providing an account of what has just happened. It means looking beneath the surface "to see and make visible and sometimes to *break open* or *break apart* the ambient stories, the stories that are already written, and to understand the relationship between the two."[23] The official narrative of the "Stanford Prison Experiment" is a story that needs breaking. Some stories about human behavior need breaking over and over again.

SOCIAL DRAMA

During the Cold War, games involving role play and simulations were very much in vogue. A new generation of experts argued that only hypothetical scenarios could help prepare for nuclear war or large-scale global conflict. Informally known as "war games," such simulations were staged as conferences or tabletop dramas with scenery and props. Participants role-played the significant actors in potential global crises. According to science historians, the "politico-military desk game" was typical of the era. It began with a crisis scenario, a stack of background papers, and some rules of engagement. Participants—usually military personnel and government officials—gathered in a conference room where they played opposing sides. A controller directed proceedings. Role plays were conducted over periods ranging from a few hours to a few days. At the close of proceedings, the materials generated were distributed to participants for feedback.[24] There was an ongoing debate as to whether role plays could generate useful new knowledge but more agreement on role play as a means of fostering engagement and empathy, particularly with people who might hold points of view different than one's own.

The boundaries of the "Stanford Prison Experiment" simulation were fuzzy, and the experiment's conditions were far from controlled. It was unclear how long the event would run. The participants playing prisoners may have experienced confusion due to the use of real-life cops and squad cars. What was the real world, and what was the as-if world of the experiment? Those playing guards were not aware that their behavior was being observed as part of the study. The violent and highly emotional interactions between prisoners and guards that emerged may well have been engendered by the experimental situation. Such criticisms, made by Krysia Yardley-Matwiejczuk and others, were extensive.

Early in his career, Zimbardo explored the attitude changes that occurred due to role play and improvisation.[25] In his view, the minimum requirements for role play were that the participant "attempted to render, sincerely and convincingly, the attitude position of another person."[26] Supported by the U.S. Army, Zimbardo's research was conducted within the Yale Attitude Change Program. It was thought that more significant attitude shifts occurred when one role-played behaviors that conflicted with one's own values. Why? Zimbardo's actual experiment had relatively low stakes. It involved students preparing a speech within brief time constraints and improvising. Or not. Unlike Milgram's, Zimbardo's early career experiments did not suggest a particular interest in dramaturgy; his focus was firmly on changing minds.

I was puzzled by the way that Zimbardo and his collaborators used terms associated with theater—such as *role play, improvisation, simulation,* and *psychodrama*—interchangeably. The title of his slideshow, for example, was "The Stanford Prison Experiment: A Simulation Study of the Psychology of Imprisonment." Krysia Yardley-Matwiejczuk, who has traced the history of role play in both research and clinical contexts in psychology, defined the practice as follows: "Role play or simulation methods are a way of deliberately constructing an approximation of aspects of a 'real-life' episode or experience, but under 'controlled conditions' . . . initiated and/or defined by the experimenter or therapist."[27] I note "controlled conditions"—this did not sound like the "Stanford Prison Experiment."

As first-year students at Adelaide University, though, we knew none of this backstory. We were tired of dusty old lectures and courses whose cutoff point for modern literature was 1930. Therefore, excitement levels were high when our international politics lecturers planned a simulation game to be staged off campus. We were each assigned to a country—with sleeping quarters and provisions to match our national economies. Our group got India, which translated to a blanket and a handful of rice to last the weekend. Well, that is how I remember it, anyway. Anger surged when we saw the Americans feasting on burgers and beer to the accompaniment of Neil Young on their cassette player. Violence broke out when "India" made a dawn raid on "America." Our lecturers were forced to intervene and call the whole thing off. My memories of the event are hazy. I do not recall the briefing documents or rules. Perhaps we played a version of the popular Inter-Nation game? I do remember, however, the intense emotions ignited by our role play.

The Brig

"Stanford Prison Experiment" consultant Carlo Prescott was not the only person interested in "prisons of the mind." During the 1960s and 1970s, there was an explosion of alternative theater groups interested in experimentation and social change. Theodore Shank, a historian of America's alternative theater scene, identified the Living Theatre, Bread and Puppet Theater, El Teatro Campesino, Robert Wilson, and Richard Foreman as some of the key players.[28] The boundaries between fiction and documentary, performers and spectators, were being blurred deliberately. Productions and performance styles designed to encourage audiences to focus on the world around them were favored. Scripts could take many forms; improvisation and less formal ways of devising play texts were common. (However, this did not mean that scripts were always authored collectively.) Jerzy Grotowski of the Polish Laboratory Theatre trained actors in a way that focused on the body's physical responses. Joseph Chaikin, director of the Open Theatre, sought to intensify the *presence* of the actor, as distinct from the *character* they were playing. International tours, teaching appointments, and residencies—including those at universities—helped disseminate and exchange ideas.

White letters against a black background read "1957 US Marine Camp Japan."[29] The light shines on a military guard as he stands, inspecting sleeping prisoners in a compound. This is Tepperman. We are watching a projected film. It is 4:30 A.M. Prisoner 2 stirs in his sleep, attracting the attention of Tepperman. Silhouetted against a light in the background, the military guard moves toward prisoner 2. The sounds of his boots as they hit the floor are ominous. The images are high contrast. Perhaps this movie was shot on the new fast 16 mm Tri-X film stock? The guard is all business now. He takes out his police baton and bashes it against the frame of the bed:

TEPPERMAN: Wake up, Two. You better move, boy.
    [Two leaps out of bed and jumps to attention.]
TWO: Yes, sir!
TEPPERMAN: You better speak low, boy, when the lights are out in the compound. You want me to wake up the other maggots? You better answer me, boy.
TWO: Yes, sir. I mean, no, sir.

Before *Punishment Park* and the "Stanford Prison Experiment," another alternative production took a prison as its performing space. In the early 1960s, the Living Theatre in New York produced Kenneth Brown's *The Brig*.[30] *The Brig*'s drama unfolded in a military prison. There was no concrete plot, only the structure of a brutal daily routine. Toward the end of its run, Jonas Mekas filmed the production (figure 5.4). The resulting film won Best Documentary at the Venice Film Festival in 1964. Many striking similarities emerge between *The Brig* and *The Stanford Prison Experiment*; the latter seems as if an amateur version of the former migrated to a purpose-built psychology laboratory.

Judith Malina and Julian Beck, partners in life as well as art, founded the Living Theatre in New York in 1948. In doing so, they helped create the experimental Off-Off-Broadway scene. Initially, the Living Theatre produced innovative plays by writers like Gertrude Stein, Jean Cocteau, T. S. Eliot, Luigi Pirandello, and Bertolt Brecht. The company's focus was experiments with poetic language that might jolt audiences into a new awareness. A new society required new images. By the 1960s, the Living Theatre was sufficiently established—if that is the right word for a decidedly antiestablishment entity—to lend support to others in the rapidly mushrooming alternative theater scene.

Playwright Kenneth Brown's script for *The Brig* was inspired by a month he spent in a penal institution in Japan as a member of the U.S. Third Marine Divi-

Figure 5.4. *The Brig*, Re:voir, 1964.

sion. Brown took careful note of the architecture and layout of the prison. This was
his starting point—so much so that he reproduced the detailed diagram that
jump-started his project at the beginning of his script. Forced to study a list of
regulations for thirty days, he decided to devise a list of rules to capture the relentless routines and feeling of oppression he endured. Key characters came next. They
were divided into two groups: guards and prisoners. The warden was central to the
first group: "In the centre of the end of the corridor was a desk where a senior sergeant known as the Warden sat. He concerned himself with the everyday running
of the place, dealing with admissions, releases, punishments and miscellaneous
problems as they rose. He was the disciplinarian and actual boss of procedure,
carrying out the instructions of his superiors." *The Brig* was described as a "concept for theatre or film."[31] Its writer specified the setting, rules, and regulations, in
addition to key dialogue and minimal dramatic action. Additional dialogue and
gestures were to be improvised. The prisoners were to be subjected to humiliation
and abuse. Day in, day out. Here is a sample of *The Brig*'s key regulations:

1. No prisoner may speak at any time except to his guards. A prisoner must
   request permission to do any and everything in the following way. "Sir,
   prisoner Number—requests permission to speak, Sir." He must speak in
   a loud, clear, impersonal, and unaffected tone ...

3. When unassigned a prisoner shall, at all times, stand at attention in front of his bunk and read *The Guidebook for Marines* . . .

7. The uniform of each prisoner should be identical.[32]

Director Judith Malina devised a similar schedule and set of rules for the rehearsal period. The regulations would inform the rehearsal.[33] Before the work began, a mimeographed sheet spelling out *The Brig* rehearsal discipline was presented to the cast. It specified break times, regulation clothing, and penalties for infraction of the rules or misconduct.[34] The latter was defined as obstructive or uncooperative behavior such as unnecessary talking, failure to follow directions, and losing costume or prop items. Failure to pass daily clothing inspections would also result in disciplinary action. The actors paid attention to accuracy, with the playwright demonstrating how to swab, how to frisk or be frisked, and even the angle at which the prison manual should be held. Critically, unlike a prison and unlike the "Stanford Prison Experiment," any actor could call for a five-minute break at any time. The boundaries between the world of the play and everyday life were clear.

The Living Theatre's production of *The Brig* placed the audience in the warden's position, watching the theater of the prisoners' lives. After seeing the play, independent filmmaker Jonas Mekas was determined to adapt it for the screen. He placed himself onstage, inside the action, with a handheld camera. His intention was not to show the play in its entirety but to catch as much of it as he could from behind the fourth wall.[35] There were some similarities between his visual approach and that of Peter Watkins. Both directors aimed for a kind of immediacy. As he watched the performance, Mekas thought to himself, "Suppose this was a real brig; suppose I was a news reporter; suppose I got permission from the US Marine Corps to go into one of their brigs and filmed the goings-on."[36] Imagining his camera as that of a newsreel, regardless of whether the events being staged could realistically have been filmed, was one of Watkins's defining methods.

Sometime in the 1960s—given the social and political upheaval of the time, perhaps it is unsurprising no one in this scene ever seems to recall precise dates—Julian Beck took a call from a reporter who needed less than fifteen words to caption a photograph of the Living Theatre. What was their purpose? After some quick consultation, Beck rang back: "To raise consciousness, to stress the sanctity of life, to bring down the walls."[37] That was the Living Theatre. *The Brig* ushered in the company's "bring down the walls" phase. When he first read the play, Beck imagined "the shouting, the marching, the stamping of feet" on the stage. A play was not simply dialogue. It encompassed design, dramatic action, choreography, music, and rhythm. The social action it might inspire was just as important as the play's dramatic action. Beck and Malina wanted the audience members to experience the brutality of prison for themselves.

As it happened, several members of *The Brig*'s cast and crew, including its playwright and cofounders, were soon behind bars themselves. The Internal Revenue Service locked the Living Theatre out of its Fourteenth Street theater due to unpaid taxes. Nevertheless, the company went ahead with its last performance of *The Brig* as planned; the audience climbing through windows and scrambling to their seats only added to the drama. Unfortunately, Living Theatre creatives soon found themselves in court facing charges of sedition. It was alleged that Beck and Malina had yelled "Storm the barricades!" to audience members waiting to enter the theater. While they were acquitted of that charge, they were convicted of several others and sentenced to a five-year suspended sentence. After its production of *The Brig*, the company went into self-imposed exile in Europe for some years. Later, it made its way to Brazil to embrace community-based theater. But that is another story.

THE "STANFORD PRISON EXPERIMENT"

During my brief time working at a lockup facility for juvenile offenders, transactional analysis was favored as a treatment model. The system was based on former U.S. Army psychiatrist Eric Berne's field guide to "games," or patterns of interaction that he saw as cover stories for people's unconscious motives. A feature of transactional analysis is a variety of diagrams that can be drawn easily in seminars. Consequently, much of our training involved whiteboards and colored markers. As residential care workers, we were to identify our young charges' "rackets" and life scripts and help them to do a rewrite. Looking back, I wonder, was this my first professional writing job?

At the end of each week, we performed a feedback exercise in which you walked around the room with a sheet of butcher paper taped to your back, and people wrote comments on your progress, or lack thereof. "Glad to get to know you!" and "You remind me of the kid sister I never had" were the kind of responses I typically attracted. As a screenwriting lecturer, I have banned butcher's paper from my seminar rooms.

On graduation day, everyone was given their long-term assignments—except me. A supervisor called me into his office to tell me they were letting me go. Apparently, I was an inappropriate authority figure. Although I could only agree with this assessment of my character and my complete lack of a future in the juvenile lockup business, I felt irrationally hurt and angry, bewildered, and dejected. We all went to the pub and drank far, far too much, and laughed and cried and promised to stay in touch. But I knew I would never see any of these people again—I had done my time.

Like *The Brig*, the "Stanford Prison Experiment" was guided by a list of rules. They were read to the prisoners. Twice.[38] Here are several of the key regulations:

1. Prisoners must remain silent during rest periods, after lights out, during meals and whenever they're outside the prison yards . . .
3. Prisoners must participate in all prison activities . . .
8. Prisoners must always address the guards as "Mr. Correctional Officer," and the Warden as "Mr. Chief Correctional Officer . . ."
15. Prisoners must obey all orders issued by guards at all times. A guard's order supersedes any written order. The Warden's order supersedes the guard's order and the written rules. Orders of the Superintendent of prisoners are supreme.

One rule specified that the prisoners must never refer to their conditions as an experiment or a simulation. This seems a surprising means of fostering immersion in a situation and role.

The selected participants were told that two problems were being studied: first, how the norms that govern behavior in a new situation developed—that is, how a psychological environment evolves within a given physical environment; and, second, how people arbitrarily assigned to play different roles experienced the same environment. Would people playing the roles of prisoner or guard behave like their real-life counterparts?

The prisoners' costume or uniform comprised a dress with a number inscribed on both the front and back. It was worn without underwear. The accessories included a heavy chain to be worn on one ankle at all times, rubber sandals, and a cap made of women's nylon stockings. The psychologist aimed to produce the humiliation and emasculation observed in real prisoners. Some professional actors build a character from the outside in, beginning with clothing and accessories. After all, these aspects of our wardrobe affect how we move and hold ourselves. Guards were provided with uniforms and mirrored sunglasses to prevent eye contact with their charges. The Stanford Prison experimenters had remarkably little awareness of issues concerning gender and behavior. The expectation was that studies involving only men could be generalized to women. This is despite the fact that one of the observations from the student-led prison simulation was that the only prisoner to rebel from beginning to end was the single female participant.

Punishment Park

A beam of light cuts through the darkness. The sounds of the 16 mm projector, housed in a makeshift control booth can be heard in the background. An assorted bunch of would-be indie filmmakers, artists, and cineastes are gathered in the former Soon Chang fireworks factory in Adelaide's East End one Sunday afternoon. It is the early 1980s, and this part of the city, near the wholesale fruit and vegetable markets, has not yet been gentrified. The smell of oranges and cabbages is never far away. Around the corner are shop fronts rented out cheaply as artists' studios. Walk down any lane, and you will spot posters advertising screenings and events—executed with widely varying degrees of skill. Activism and art belonged together. Those dense networks of lanes connect community organizations devoted to women's art, experimental art, film, and video art. This is where I learned about the films of Peter Watkins.

Black and white. Air-raid sirens sound. We are inside a house near Kent in England. The year is unspecified. A middle-class family of four rush to move furniture against the walls. Their tea things are still on the table: a teapot, cups, and a half-eaten plate of scones. A warden seizes pictures from the walls as she strips the room of breakables: "Come on, children!" The camera, swooping around the room, captures the sense of urgency. We can never quite grasp the full picture. A BBC-style narrator cuts in, his tone ominous: "this could be the last two minutes of peace in Britain." The sirens crescendo. The camera follows a soldier as he jogs to the next house. A window bursts into flames. Out on the street, we cut to the moments following a nuclear explosion. The pictures are solarized—they look like photographic negatives flooded with light. Two men are up against a wall, doubled over in pain and coughing. The narrator lists their symptoms in clinical detail. You get the picture.

Peter Watkins first hit the headlines with his explosive film *The War Game* in 1965.[39] Originally commissioned for the BBC's "Wednesday Play" slot, *The War Game* blended reportage, interviews, and narration to create a newsreel of an imagined event: a nuclear attack on Britain by the Soviet Union. Depicting harrowing scenes of firestorms, radiation sickness, and the breakdown of law and order, the film was banned from being broadcast due to government pressure. Eventually screened in cinemas, *The War Game* won the 1966 Academy Award for Best Documentary Feature. It was one of a series of films in which Watkins created a "you are there" style of newsreel immediacy. His purpose was "to involve ordinary people in an extended study of their own history" (albeit, in the case of *The War Game*, histories imagined as just over the horizon).[40] Watkins, who began his career in amateur film clubs, developed a distinctive method of working with nonprofessional actors. Casting was conducted via a series of public meetings held in towns throughout Kent. Most of the film, including scenes of the firestorm, was shot in a disused military barracks. Interview subjects were also played by nonprofessional actors who delivered verbatim quotes. These stylized interviews featured political and religious figures in favor of nuclear war alongside doctors and psychiatrists who provided evidence about the likely human fallout.

Watkins described the origins of his later film *Punishment Park* like this. In 1970, he was in the United States researching and preparing a feature documentary on the Civil War. However, the project was unable to obtain financing (an

Figure 5.5. *Punishment Park*, Project X, 1971.

all-too-familiar story for most filmmakers). He then considered making a film reconstructing the trial of political activists, the Chicago Seven, and was offered funds for an ultra-low-budget production. While casting this film, Watkins met various people who had been arrested at Vietnam War protests. He found their stories especially vivid. At roughly the same time, the director discovered the Internal Security Act of 1950 (64 Stat. 987). "This draconian legislation allowed for the setting up of places of detention . . . for those accused by the government of dissidence," he recalled.[41] Set in the near future, *Punishment Park* envisaged a new legal system introduced to deal with the rising numbers of people convicted at demonstrations opposing the Vietnam War. The social drama featured three groups: prisoners, police, and tribunal. A fictional newsreel crew followed their every move.

Open casting sessions were held in local halls and attracted large numbers of interested participants. The film cuts between two related story lines. As prisoners struggle to cross the desert with law enforcement officers in hot pursuit, a civilian emergency tribunal meets in a large tent. Its role is to judge and sentence the next group of dissidents (figure 5.5). Cinematographer Joan Churchill circled and moved around the actors; she aimed to cover the drama in multiple areas by panning or zooming, adjusting the focus on the fly. These strategies also added a sense of immediacy. The newsreel quality of the film was enhanced by desaturating the color and using diffusion filters to create a softer-edged image. Essentially, Watkins staged a large-scale dramatic conflict in the desert and, in collaboration with his crew, prepared strategies to shoot the event as it unfolded.

Known for his ability to elicit strong performances from nonprofessional actors, Watkins saw his *Punishment Park* cast as falling into two categories: those expressing their own views, and those playing characters whose opinions they opposed. Ultimately, said Watkins, everyone possesses the ability to improvise. His role was to encourage the actors to express themselves as freely as possible and heighten the reality of the situation. There were no rehearsals; instead, the cast prepared by working on their characters' backgrounds and the ways they might express their political positions: "All that mattered was that the person came across as a real person and not as someone acting."[42] If someone spoke only two lines, it was nonsense to spend time going into their character's background and personality. The actors were not playing individual people; rather, they represented people in a particular set of circumstances. For Watkins, character concerned the social and political dimensions of life rather than individual traits and emotions. *Punishment Park* was an experiment in political cinema.

Peter Watkins credited the Brazilian playwright, director, and thinker Augusto Boal as a key influence. Boal, who trained as an engineer at Columbia University, returned to his homeland at the invitation of São Paulo's Arena Theatre. He wore his politics on his sleeve from the beginning. *Revolucao na America do Sul (Revolution in South America)*, produced in 1961 from Boal's script, was seen as introducing a new era of political protest theater. Oppression, according to Boal, occurred when one person was dominated by the monologue of another and had no chance to reply. Gradually, he developed a community-based method of devising and directing theater. Legend has it that an audience member once leaped onto the stage to demonstrate a suggestion to the actor. Boal began inviting audiences with suggestions for changes to interrupt the action and do the same. In 1971, during the military dictatorship in Brazil, while walking home from the theater, Boal was kidnapped, jailed, and tortured. On his release, he went into exile. Prisons were among the many places in which he later taught. In the belief that both groups were oppressed, he worked with guards and prisoners.

The work of many socially engaged alternative and community-based theater makers of the 1960s and 1970s, and independent filmmakers such as Mekas and Watkins, saw a blurring of the boundaries between research and scripting, drama and documentary, professional and nonprofessional performers, and audience and spectators. There was a desire to look beyond conventional notions of individual characters and their journeys—what Anne Bogart called drama about "you, me, our apartment and our problems"—a hunger for immediacy and a desire to speak to the issues of the time.[43] Rather than separate art forms,

categorized according to media, such performance-based works should perhaps be grouped broadly as social drama.

Zimbardo involved the media in his simulation from the very beginning.
As volunteers were rounded up on the streets and arrested, they were filmed
by a local broadcaster. The report made that evening's news. For audiences,
too, the boundaries between reality and artifice were muddled. If Zimbardo
enthusiastically embraced broadcast media, Watkins despaired of it. Many of
his films are critiques of the media and, in particular, the story template he
calls the "mono-form"—rapidly cut images and sounds moving toward a predetermined conclusion.[44] This form dominated both Hollywood and broadcast
media and allowed little room for audience reflection.

The "Stanford Prison Experiment," *The Brig*, and *Punishment Park* were all
dramas of the 1960s and 1970s, structured around the brutal daily routines of
prison settings. We might criticize the "Stanford Prison Experiment" for its lack
of rigor and excessive hype, but it would be a mistake to dismiss it as a "happening" or "guerrilla theater." Implicit in this term is science's disdain for the arts.
The productions of the Living Theatre, Peter Watkins, and Augusta Boal all share
a deep commitment to art, social action, and the renewal of visual and theatrical language. Their works posed questions about how citizens might respond to
the social and political challenges of their times. Zimbardo and his collaborators claimed the validity of science but none of its rigor.

CHAPTER 6

Crime Scenes

"It is Sunday August 14, 1971, 9.55 A.M. The temperature is in the seventies, the humidity is low, as usual, the visibility is unlimited: there is a cloudless azure blue sky above. Another postcard-perfect summer day begins in Palo Alto, California."[1] This is how Philip Zimbardo recalled the opening of the "Stanford Prison Experiment" (the event, not the movie). *The Lucifer Effect: How Good People Turn Evil*, his lengthy eyewitness account, was published more than three decades later. As soon as I read that "visibility was unlimited," I knew we were entering the world of myth. After all, Zimbardo was recalling the event from a distance of more than thirty years.

The year 1971. Trouble was brewing. Tune in to the news, and you would have learned that the Vietnam War dragged on, antiwar and civil rights demonstrators were out on the streets, and Black Panther George Jackson was about to go to court for the murder of a prison officer. (In fact, Zimbardo was preparing to appear as an expert witness for Jackson's defense.) In cities across America, social unrest and violence were on the rise.

On the Sunday morning in question, a real-life police car cruised the streets of Palo Alto, picking up those students who had agreed to participate in a psychology experiment. Zimbardo and the graduate student who would play the role of prison warden tailed the police car. The officers were asked to drive slowly for the benefit of a local television news crew on board. Once the police arrested the "suspects" and delivered them to a holding cell at the local station, Zimbardo and his warden took over. They blindfolded their prisoners—or should I say hostages?—and drove them to a mock jail in the basement of Stanford University's psychology building.[2]

The Hollywood screenplay templates popularized by gurus such as Syd Field and Robert McKee begin with an inciting incident that sets the story in motion—complications will follow. The incident can be as monumental as an explosion in a Hollywood movie or as seemingly inconsequential as the arrival of the next guest in the British television comedy series *Fawlty Towers*.[3] In Zimbardo's rewrite of his "Stanford Prison Experiment," aligning it more closely with these screenplay templates, the Sunday morning arrests formed the inciting incident.

From the beginning, the boundaries between the real and the imaginary were fuzzy. The use of blindfolds, for example, was not standard police procedure. Their use was intended to disorient the students, thus making them more compliant. By Zimbardo's account, at first, neither the local police nor broadcasters were keen to participate. However, Zimbardo had been associated with the Yale University psychology department's Attitude Change research team. He reeled the television station in first. Little that was newsworthy generally happened on a Sunday; therefore, they would have at least one segment in the bag by covering the arrests. When the producer agreed, Zimbardo sold the story to the police as a public relations exercise.[4]

Smashed Windows

This was not Zimbardo's first brush with crime. He explicitly linked the "Stanford Prison Experiment" to a demonstration about vandalizing cars staged two years earlier. This earlier experiment formed the backstory.[5] In May 1969, the then-thirty-six-year-old psychology professor issued a press release drawing attention to a grab bag of his recent experiments exploring violence and deindividuation—that is, the loss of individual identity in groups. The *San Francisco Examiner* devoted a feature article to the man considered one of social psychology's rising stars.[6] (Brief reports also appeared in other daily newspapers and *Time* magazine.)[7] Two of Zimbardo's "chilling laboratory experiments" attracted the most interest: the abandoned automobile experiment and the hooded girls.

Let us start with the first crime—or, rather, a misdemeanor. As *Time* magazine reported, "At 3:15 on a recent Friday afternoon, a 1959 green Oldsmobile is parked alongside the curb in the middle-class residential neighborhood of New York City. Two men got out, removed the license plates, and opened the hood slightly to make the car look as if it had been stolen and left."[8] Although the suspects had been captured on camera, the police were not making inquiries. The reveal? The two shady-looking characters were not criminals but social psychologists.

In a *Candid Camera*–inspired experiment, Zimbardo and his research assistant abandoned the car on a city street.[9] Taking cover, they conducted a stakeout, observing and recording the action via written logs and a hidden camera. What the psychologists saw shocked them. Over three days, and in nearly two dozen separate incidents, people stripped the Oldsmobile of any items of value, including the tires, battery, and radiator. Then, the smashing began. The culprits usually operated in teams. These were not gangs of teenagers but rather middle-class couples and families. One man even enlisted his son to act as a lookout. People who passed by did not intervene. It is easy to imagine the scene as a time lapse featuring a succession of ordinary citizens hauling away spare parts at high speed as the sun rose, cast its shadows on the sidewalks, and fell below the horizon. However, the standard *Candid Camera*-style punch line was missing. No one stepped out from the shadows to ask, "Aren't people funny?" This skit took a darker turn—it was evidence of the dehumanization of urban life, said Zimbardo—big-city senseless violence.

In the next scenario, a matching vehicle was abandoned on campus at Stanford University. Again, Zimbardo and his team stepped back to observe the action. Remarkably, though, no one vandalized the car in California. The researchers were eventually forced to make a start themselves. Then all hell broke loose. "It feels so good after the first smack, then the next one feels easy . . . and the next feels even better," one participant said.[10] However, the article fails to reveal that this quote was from Zimbardo himself. "One student jumped on the roof and began stomping it in, two were pulling the door from its hinges, another hammered away at the hood, while the last one broke all the glass he could find."[11] It was only then that bystanders were persuaded to join in.

Zimbardo linked his automobile experiment to a litany of crimes and statistics. In 1967, vandals in New York City had smashed 202,712 school windows. In San Francisco, that same year, approximately 100,000 windows were smashed in buildings in local parks alone. A crowd of 200 students at the University of Oklahoma yelled, "Jump, jump, jump," until a disturbed man did just that, leaping from a building to his death.[12] This strategy of associating psychology's field tests—most often short, dramatic scenarios staged on the streets—with signal crimes was successfully employed to promote the bystander effect theory. Experimenters pointed to what we now know to be a false story about the rape and murder of New Yorker Kitty Genovese. I was beginning to feel like a fact-checker. As soon as I saw that "200 students" supposedly yelled, "Jump," I suspected there was more to the story.

Diving into an archive, I looked for newspaper reports of likely incidents. On September 27, 1967, a thirty-nine-year-old man named Fred Green made his way onto the University of Oklahoma campus.[13] Green, who had a history of mental illness, had admitted himself voluntarily to a psychiatric hospital earlier that week. On the evening in question, Green ate dinner at 6:15 P.M. and caught a taxi to the university. Climbing onto the roof of a twelve-story building, he prepared to jump. A small crowd soon gathered; the numbers were not reported. A verbal exchange between Green and some students followed. A few were alleged to have taunted him. Others helped by fetching police and trying to talk the suicidal man down. Sadly, Green jumped to his death. This reads like another bystander story. After all, the narrative of bystander indifference had been well established by

1967, and social scientists were actively searching for new insights. In this incident, the students were presented as having actively inflamed the situation. However, what we know of the actual event suggests more complex contributing
factors and triggers. Nuanced accounts do not always allow blame to be so readily
apportioned.

A decade earlier, Gordon Parks, the first African American staff photographer at *Life* magazine, attempted to provide a more complex account of crime
in cities. Parks was assigned to a project with the working title "Crime in the U.S."
Accompanying police officers on patrol in New York, Chicago, San Francisco, and
Los Angeles for six weeks, Park took more than 300 color photographs. Twelve
images, some of them cropped, were published in the magazine with the title
"Atmosphere of Crime." Journalist Robert Wallace wrote the accompanying text.[14]

"The nation in the fall of 1957 appears to be threatened by a catastrophic wave
of crime. From almost every major city in the past year have come frightening
reports showing not merely an increase in the number of crimes but a dreadful
shift, it seems, in their nature."[15] The opening lines of Wallace's narrative played
into societal fears of the time. In 2020, New York's Museum of Modern Art
exhibited several of Park's "Atmosphere of Crime" photographs for the first time.
Viewed without the original accompanying text, they tell a different story.[16]

In "Atmosphere of Crime," Parks provides a double portrait of the criminal
justice system and the individuals caught up within it. We follow police and officials as they go out on patrol, cruise the city, make arrests, conduct interviews,
complete routine paperwork, and visit morgues and prisons. Most crime photographers shot in black and white and attempted to show the perpetrator's face.
Parks, who made use of color film and available light, shot the alleged criminals
from unexpected angles, in shadow, and with blur to "allow the suspect a degree
of anonymity, some dignity," says photography curator Sarah Meisner.[17] His palette for "Atmosphere of Crime" skewed to smoky blues, greens, and browns.
Splashes of light against midnight blue skies provided contrast. Parks human-
ized his subjects. Providing glimpses of a largely hidden world, his intensely cinematic images challenged stereotypes of criminality that were pervasive in the
mainstream media. According to Meisner, Park's series complicates our sense
of crime: "If we look at this scene and find ourselves *anticipating* a crime, we have
to ask ourselves why that is. Is it because it's a poor neighborhood? Because it's
at night? Is it because guys are hanging out on the corner? But where's the crime
in that?"[18]

The promotion for Zimbardo's work went further than any one incident (or
cluster of incidents, such as the four cited by Darley and Latane to support their
bystander effect, discussed in chapter 4), linking his experiments to increased
incidents of rape, violence against children, soaring incarceration rates, and murders. These numbers were evidence of an increasingly violent United States—all

the result of deindividuation. Living in big cities, we feel anonymous, Zimbardo claimed. Consequently, we are more likely to break the social contract that binds people into communities.

A decade or two later, social scientists and politicians took the image of the broken window and ran with it. Zimbardo's automobile vandalism experiment was used as the key empirical evidence for the "broken windows" theory devised by James Wilson and George Kelling in the early 1980s. "If a window in a building is broken and is left unrepaired, all the rest of the windows will soon be broken," they wrote.[19] The theory seemed intuitive. Visible signs of decay, such as broken windows, graffiti, or people loitering on the streets, signaled that no one cared. This theory applied to "nice" and run-down neighborhoods alike. Zimbardo's automobile vandalism experiment was invoked as evidence—it had tested the broken windows theory; crucially, however, the theory was not developed until long after the vandalism field test. The solution was simple—if police focused on maintaining order by patrolling neighborhoods on foot, major crime would soon decrease. New York City politicians seized on the idea. Elections were fought and won based on new law enforcement strategies. As the number of violent crimes committed in New York City dropped, local officials celebrated a success story.

However, cracks soon appeared in the story. Social policy scholars Bernard Harcourt and Jens Ludwig ran some numbers of their own. Crime statistics had fallen not only in New York City but also in many other American cities where "broken window" policing was not in place.[20] Additionally, fixing broken windows had morphed into the racist "stop and frisk" policy.[21] Built on shaky foundations, the "broken window" story was too good to be true. More social scientists and journalists weighed in; eventually, the policy was discredited. Some argued that Zimbardo's vandalism experiment had been misrepresented through oversimplification.[22] Linking the image of the broken window to violent crime simplified complex issues regarding the safety of neighborhoods. Who was responsible for keeping communities safe? Ordinary citizens? Or the police? How could they work together? Given the history of racist policing, could they ever work together? But I am not a criminologist. What interests me is Zimbardo's talent for crafting the telling metaphor—his facility with word pictures.

Despite my father's profession, I have little personal experience of crime. As university students, my friend Z and I were caught one night spray-painting slogans on the side of a row of vacant houses. Our solution to inner-city dwellings abandoned during a housing crisis was to propose that people squat in them. Down the road was the city's first shelter for women and kids seeking refuge from domestic violence. Our clothes were almost permanently splattered with paint due to weekends spent getting places into shape for those ready to move in. There was never enough affordable housing available. "Don't let houses rot, squat," we were writing in red paint when a local police patrol caught us in the glare of its headlights. Somewhat inept at our task, Z and I panicked and misspelled the word *houses* (adding an extra "es") while the police waited to take our details and charge us. Courtesy of our involvement in local community and political groups, we were represented by one of the city's leading barristers, and the charges were dismissed. The most traumatic part of our brush with crime was the straight clothes that the barrister insisted we wear to court. My skirt and blouse were borrowed from my sister, and I think Z's father gave him a tie.

The teenage kids we worked with at the community project did not fare nearly so well. They were routinely picked up by the police and placed in institutions for juvenile offenders. Often, their offenses could be traced to running away from the latest in a succession of group foster homes. Hunger and boredom soon led to minor pilfering or damage to property. When it came to the law, they did not share our privileges and were rarely given the benefit of the doubt or assumed to be of good character.

Caught by a newsreel camera, a protester runs toward a shop front window and raises an arm. Ready to lob a rock or a bomb? That image of broken windows covers protest, rebellion, war, riots, urban crime, and more. Suffragettes breaking windows with toffee hammers in early twentieth-century London. Kristallnacht in Germany in 1938, when the windows of Jewish-owned shops were smashed. The broken windows of bombed-out buildings in London during World War II. A burglar sneaking in via a window in a 1940s detective movie. Kids throwing stones at the windows of abandoned buildings. The race riots of 1960s America. Eventually, George Kelling—one of the architects of the "broken window" policy—called time: "We didn't know how powerful it was going to be. It simplified, it was easy to communicate, a lot of people got it. . . . But, as you know, metaphors can wear out and become stale."[23] Exactly.

What makes ideas sticky? This is the question social scientists and marketing gurus Dan and Chip Heath asked themselves. The brothers eventually came up with a list of principles. Sticky ideas were simple, unexpected, credible, concrete, and engaged the emotions. There was an acronym to sell the Heaths' idea, of course—"SUCCES." The last "S" stood for "stories." Forget statistics—sticky ideas were always expressed as stories.

Like many landmark experiments in social psychology, the "Stanford Prison Experiment" ticks most of those boxes. It was simple, unexpected in its era, credible because its experimenter was a professor of social psychology at a highly regarded university, concrete, and engaged the emotions. These were mostly negative—fear, shame, distress, humiliation, and anger were among the emotions reported. If you had to reduce the Heath brothers' list of principles to its essence, you would end up with simple stories. But why would you want to convince people of ideas about human behavior that might be wrong?

HOODED GIRLS

A black-and-white photograph depicts three New York University students wearing what look like paper bags over their heads. Openings have been cut for eyes and mouths.[24] The photo was printed using high contrast; the hooded figures appear to emerge from an inky pool of darkness. This image, published two years before the "Stanford Prison Experiment," helped establish its visual iconography. Before the mock prison, Zimbardo ran a torture study. Small groups of girls, some wearing hoods, listened to sound recordings of a fellow student speaking. Then, they were placed in a dark cubicle and asked to administer electric shocks to a victim—the young woman they had just heard speak. Those wearing hoods were more likely to inflict shocks than those who were unhooded, Zimbardo reported. In one version, the victim was described as either "nice" or "obnoxious." (Yes, gender stereotyping was alive and well.) When the young woman's personality was described as obnoxious, the hooded girls pressed the buzzer more often and for longer. Again, this represented deindividuation. In another huge leap from evidence to real life, Zimbardo claimed, "Under the right conditions every one of us is an assassin."[25]

We are watching a silent film. Figures in white hoods gather at night, a burning cross in the background. Violence is in the air. This is a scene from D. W. Griffith's *The Birth of a Nation*, depicting the white supremacist Ku Klux Klan.[26] The controversial film is often described as Hollywood's first realist masterpiece due to the artistry with which its director staged large-scale dramatic action. I have never been able to accept that *The Birth of a Nation* deserves those accolades. Historical document? Yes. Art? Not for me. Surely, art connects people, brings us together? The photograph of the hooded girls in Zimbardo's torture experiment derives some of its shock value from the association with the Ku Klux Klan.

I recall another black-and-white image of figures with covered faces, this time from the world of art photography. Standing in a park, a group of people face the camera wearing paper bags over their heads. Toward the end of her life, photographer Diane Arbus visited homes for intellectually disabled women to take portraits. She preferred to make her visits during holidays when the residents were often excited—there were enough pictures of unhappy people in institutional settings. Arbus shot portraits with the consent of her subjects, who posed as they wished. The lexicon of photography makes it hard to discuss this kind of negotiation. Terms like *subject*, *shot*, and *capture* do not seem adequate to the task. The image that I recall is most likely *Untitled (4)*, in which four women are dressed for a Halloween party. It is not quite as I remember. Some of the women wear paper bags, and others wear masks, adding to the unsettling effect. The portraits are full length, indicating that, as usual, Arbus kept her distance—four feet, to be precise.

The artist gravitated toward subjects who lived at the fringes of society. Should the subjects of portraits be consulted about their exhibition or publication? What constituted informed consent? Psychology does not have a monopoly on ethical dilemmas and lapses. As a student, I pored over Arbus's photographs. It was only later that I fully appreciated the photographer's technique. Arbus experimented with slow shutter speeds to achieve the right mix of sharp focus and blurred background and combined flashlight with daylight. Then she discovered working with early afternoon winter sunlight. "Perfect," she wrote. This light gave the series a floating quality. *Untitled (4)* is unsettling—but aren't photographs of people with hoods or bags over their heads always unsettling?

We can often trace the decisions made by photographers like Diane Arbus.[27] Far from snap judgments, they were often documented in notebooks or journals. Psychology frequently treats the camera as a neutral recording device rather than an instrument of discovery. Consequently, details of the images produced rarely make it into experimenters' laboratory notebooks. Zimbardo's photographs of the torture experiments from 1969 could be called *Unknown*. The subjects are, of course, not identified to protect their identities. But who was behind the camera? Routinely attributed to experimenters, in the 1960s and 1970s, such photographs were more likely taken by university audiovisual technical staff. Choices of camera, lens, film stock, angle, and shutter speed are just some of the factors that shape photographs. A color print from Zimbardo's torture experiments, for example, offers another layer of information, another mood. In comparison with the high-contrast black-and-white shots, more detail can be seen. The paper bags over the girls' heads are covered with patterns that resemble camouflage.[28] The drama is dialed down, and the military associations made clearer.

HOODED MAN

In 2004, when stories of prisoner abuse at Abu Ghraib prison, Iraq, hit the headlines, the "Stanford Prison Experiment" was back in the news. A series of "trophy shots" taken by U.S. military personnel showed grinning soldiers standing over piles of naked prisoners and detainees being forced to perform demeaning sexual acts. If millions of words have been devoted to the "Stanford Prison Experiment," zillions of pixels have (deservedly) been devoted to discussion of the photographs of Abu Ghraib prison. Among the thousands of photographs taken, one of the most well known is "Hooded Man," which shows a prisoner wearing a hood and standing on a box with electrodes attached to his fingers. He was forced to stand on the box and told that he would be electrocuted if he fell off. The image has been described by *Time* magazine as among the 100 most significant photographs of all time.[29]

When Sergeant Joseph Derby blew the whistle, passing on a disc containing a selection of the Abu Ghraib prison images to a superior officer, the wide-scale torture and abuse could no longer be ignored. Zimbardo claimed that he was unsurprised by the behavior of Abu Ghraib prison guards. They were swaggering and sadistic, placing bags over the prisoners' heads, forcing them to strip naked, and forcing them to perform sexual acts. He had seen it all before. There were strikingly parallel pictures from the "Stanford Prison Experiment."[30] One photograph from Stanford shows "inmates" with bags over their heads waiting in a corridor for their parole hearing. (In the experiment's fictional world, prisoners could only be released after making an appearance before the board.) The tough guy guard, dubbed "John Wayne" by the experimenters, leans toward the prisoners. This is not a particularly menacing image; it is the psychologist's narration that endeavors to make it so. It was also Zimbardo who initially produced the idea of covering prisoners' heads with bags for his role play. Photographs of Abu Ghraib prison detainees with hoods or paper bags over their heads allowed Zimbardo an opportunity to link the "Stanford Prison Experiment" to yet another real-world event, thereby bringing his work to the attention of a new generation. He soon stepped forward as an expert witness for the defense.

The anonymity of the victim in "Hooded Man" gave the photograph much of its power. Various claims were put forward and investigated, but ultimately the person chose to remain unnamed. However, the photographer's identity was no secret. Senior Staff Sergeant Ivan "Chip" Fredericks took the most widely published "Hooded Man" photograph. It was taken with a Sony Cyber-shot digital camera on November 4, 2003, at 11:03 P.M.[31] A cell phone shot taken three minutes later shows Fredericks checking his camera as the unknown hooded man holds the stress position. Fredericks later faced trial on multiple charges, including maltreatment of detainees. Photography critic and former New York Times picture editor Fred Ritchin observed that, during the Vietnam War, the most compelling imagery was taken by professional photographers. By contrast, it was the photographs taken by soldiers in Iraq that became inscribed in collective memory.[32]

After reviewing the available records and conducting interviews, Zimbardo concluded that there was "absolutely nothing in his record . . . that would predict that Chip Frederick would engage in any form of abusive, sadistic behavior."[33] It was Specialist Charles Graner (a U.S. Army reservist) who took charge on the night that the "Hooded Man" photographs were taken—he was the ringleader. Fredericks was the "good apple" in the situation, and Graner the "bad apple." As an expert witness for the defense, Zimbardo significantly underplayed the torture and violence directed at Abu Ghraib prison inmates. It served his interest to highlight any possible similarities between his role play and the U.S.-run military prison. However, unlike the fictional Stanford Prison, Abu Ghraib prison was only too real—a place where real crimes, including rape, torture, and murder, were routine. Zimbardo testified that Fredericks bore no responsibility; the situation alone was to blame.[34] "Give me an image of the all-American boy, and it's this young man," said Zimbardo. "He is a wonderful young man who did these horrible things."[35] A prison officer before his stint as a military policeman at Abu Ghraib prison, Frederick was thirty-seven years old.

"History itself is a crime scene and you're the detective," said Errol Morris.[36] Filmmaking is a tool for solving some of the mysteries. Morris, who started out as a private investigator, has brought that sensibility to a significant body of film work. On the cusp of drama and documentary, his films take nonfiction in a decidedly forensic direction. Increasingly, photography, truth, and the nature of evidence have become the subjects of his investigations.[37] Morris's feature documentary *Standard Operating Procedure* (2008) focused on key photographs from Abu Ghraib prison in the belief that photography offers a different window into history.[38] The filmmaker interviewed soldiers who had worked at Abu Ghraib prison using his Interrotron device. Inspired by the teleprompter, Morris's invention allows interviewees to address a floating image near the camera—either the interviewer or a piece of evidence under discussion. Thus, subjects appear to look straight at the camera as they speak.[39] The Interrotron machine may be seen as a modern-day version of the lie detector machines with which early psychology and cinema were both enamored.

"Photographs reveal and conceal," stated Morris.[40] The first-person testimonies in *Standard Operating Procedure* were interwoven with re-enactments of key photographs from Abu Ghraib prison. They were shot on a studio set constructed to appear as an endless corridor. Many of the soldiers' photographs were staged in a corridor that became a performance space. For all the skill and visual flair of Morris's photographic re-enactments, watching *Standard Operating Procedure* is a reminder that cinematic re-enactments do not provide conclusive evidence; rather, they highlight investigative working theories or possible leads. Why were the photographs taken? Whose interests are served?

The debate regarding *Standard Operating Procedure* has been fierce. Critiquing the film, documentary theorist Bill Nichols wrote that "my sense of a social order depends on accountability and responsibility of the one to the many and of the many to the one."[41] Morris's almost clinical investigation of the states of mind of those guards who took the Abu Ghraib photographs evaded questions of responsibility. Moreover, where were the voices of the Iraqi detainees who were depicted being tortured and abused? How was it conscionable to re-enact such scenes without presenting their perspective? Drawing our attention to the digitally created white frames with which Morris surrounds the photographs, film theorist Linda Williams offers a different view: the "minimalist white frames, endlessly multiplied, point to the characterizations of digital mediation at work."[42] They invite us to consider the act of witnessing the photographs.

Errol Morris dismissed attempts to draw on the "Stanford Prison Experiment" or Milgram's "Obedience to Authority" to account for the dynamics of Abu Ghraib prison; you did not need psychology experiments to tell you why those in the military followed orders—they were trained to do so. This ignores the fact that Milgram's experiment provides as much evidence of resistance as obedience. Surprisingly, some of Morris's conclusions were not so different from those of Zimbardo. Abu Ghraib prison was a situation not of the soldiers' making, and they were not responsible for their conduct. Morris acknowledged, however, that the story surrounding the Abu Ghraib prison images is extremely complex.

Zimbardo first began discussing the "Stanford Prison Experiment" with a slide-tape show designed as a teaching package. The first iteration comprised eighty slides, and an accompanying audiocassette contained Zimbardo's scripted commentary and sound grabs. The story was told primarily from his vantage point as prison superintendent and principal investigator. The dramatic effect was heightened by adding "photos and sounds from the 'real world,' real prisons, real concentration camps and military installations."[43] They included Margaret Bourke-White's photographs of concentration camps and a montage of news headlines about riots at Attica Prison in 1971. The story was expanded after Zimbardo appeared in 2004 as a witness for Frederick's defense, and the real-life images drawn on to support Zimbardo's prison simulation findings shifted from Attica Prison to Abu Ghraib prison. "The more an image is joined with other things, the more often it *flourishes*. The more an image is joined with other things, the more ways in which it can be *excited*," said artist and critic John Berger, quoting Spinoza.[44] This provides an apt description of Zimbardo's aspirations as he linked the "Stanford Prison Experiment" story and its photographs with as many real-life events as possible.

"To look is an act of choice," says Berger. "We never look at just one thing; we are always looking at the relation between things and ourselves. Our vision is continually active, continually moving, continually holding things in a circle around itself."[45] If anything, images are even more open-ended and ambiguous than words. They cannot be reduced to a set of fixed meanings; context, that world outside the frame, is everything.

Stories—and the vivid pictures that bring them to life—act on the world. One disturbing aspect of the Stanford prison simulation is that it has been used consistently to excuse those who have abused others, but rarely in the service of the abused. Why, then, does the story keep being told? Surely, one major factor is that it effectively taps into societal fears. Zimbardo's experiments always place ordinary citizens, including himself, at the crime scene. His expert testimony lets us off the hook—good people will always turn bad.

It was a quiet Sunday morning in Palo Alto on August 14, 1971, and visibility was unlimited.

But was it?

CHAPTER 7

Restaging the Psychology Experiment

If psychology fell in love with the movies, can it also be said that film and television fell in love with the psychology experiment? In recent decades, key experiments have proved fertile ground for film and program makers—none more so than Milgram's "Obedience to Authority" and Zimbardo's "Stanford Prison Experiment." Both involved ordinary citizens placed under enormous stress, and both dramatized complex questions about how we negotiate issues of obedience and authority and make decisions to resist or accede to social pressure. People would not believe what had occurred unless they saw it with their own eyes. In both cases, footage filmed via hidden cameras provided evidence, and those visual records were critical in attracting media interest.

Compared with "Obedience to Authority" and the "Stanford Prison Experiment," other social psychology experiments of the postwar era lacked an underlying dramatic scenario that could be adapted and repurposed. This was often the case despite the fact that the social issues under investigation remained only too pertinent. Solomon Asch's series of experiments on conformity and independence, for example, arguably offered a more nuanced account of social behavior than Milgram's "Obedience to Authority." But they lacked human drama. After all, which of the following scenarios would you prefer to watch: young men choosing the longest line on a piece of paper or people facing pressure to inflict an electric shock on an innocent person? Milgram had worked with Asch as a research assistant. "I was trying to think of a way to make Asch's conformity experiments more humanly significant. I was dissatisfied that the test of conformity was a judgement about lines," said Milgram.[1] The bystander effect scenarios devised by John Darley and his collaborators in the late 1960s addressed an important social issue—when do people not help others?—but the scenarios lacked narrative complexity and build.

This chapter examines screen projects that have adapted Milgram's "Obedi-ence to Authority" experiments, including my own. These projects span feature films, factual programs for broadcast, documentary films, and gallery installa-tions. Their directors variously describe their works as "re-enactments," "reprises," or "dramatizations." What is meant by these terms? And what are their respec-tive claims to the truth? My hunch is that they are just that—claims. If we accept that Milgram's "Obedience to Authority" experiments are a drama, they are all new productions of a classic text I am going to call *Obedience: A Drama*. This text encompasses Milgram's production notes, scripted lines, and key elements of his production design.

Theater director Katie Mitchell has suggested that each production of a clas-sic text explores several key ideas.[2] In doing so, Mitchell distinguishes between a concept—which she sees as an overarching idea a director imposes on the production—and the working ideas explored by the director and cast. Mitchell has a reputation for combining aesthetic experimentation with rigorous textual analysis. For most of the work she stages, there is no living writer who can be consulted. Therefore, the director advocates discovering some basics about the writer and the society in which they lived. What are the points of connection between the play and the writer's life? List some key images, she suggests. How do they shed light on the ideas of the play? Working ideas must be able to be expressed clearly and simply: "An idea must have a relationship with nearly every character in the play and large chunks of the action must be concerned with investigating this idea."[3] For example, when she first read Chekhov's play *The Seagull*, Mitchell was struck by how many of its characters were unhappy in love. Investigating the key ideas of a dramatic text also involves consideration of genre and style. Each text has its own history and logic that help define the world depicted and how its characters interact. Realism, horror, absurdism, the Theatre of Cruelty, and black comedy—these are just some of the genres within which Milgram's "Obedience to Authority" drama could be restaged.

Re-enactment

At his desk, the Experimenter organizes his papers. The Teacher faces the shock machine. He appears bewildered by its complex arrangement of switches. We hear the Experimenter's familiar instruction, "Please begin." Reflections of the gallery audience can be seen in the glass windows of the laboratory. Long before making my own film, I read about *The Milgram Re-enactment*, first performed at the Centre for Contemporary Art, Glasgow, in 2002.[4] Watching a video doc-umenting the event, I register the familiar laboratory. Rod Dickinson and his collaborators created a facsimile of Milgram's laboratory set to scale, including a replica of the original shock machine.

Contemporary productions—viewed in color, rather than in black and white—restore Milgram's laboratory set to shades of green and white. Milgram took some trouble with the chromatic aspects of design, writing to paint manufacturers for professional color charts and advice. The hue he eventually selected for the walls is an "institutional green," one of a range of viridescent shades popularized by color consultant Faber Birren, who set up an influential color consulting business in New York in the 1930s. Birren recommended pale greens for use in public institutions for their supposedly calming effect. So ubiquitous was the use of institutional green in the postwar period that it has now accrued additional layers of meaning associated with conformity and monotony. A mere glimpse of the color makes me want to run for my life.

Curator Vivienne Gaskin, who commissioned the work, described *The Milgram Re-enactment* as a mirror image of the original.[5] Its script was based on eight transcripts sourced from the Stanley Milgram Papers archived at Yale University. According to Dickinson, he did not set out to prove or disprove Milgram's thesis or to generate new scientific data. The role of art galleries was to create spaces to observe and consider the processes of representation and remediation: "The original experiment was laden with artifice. . . . The reenactment set up a further set of iterations through time and space; actors playing the role of actors, the repetition of the experiment as a live performance eight times in real time."[6] Dickinson was interested in Milgram's use of dramaturgy in a science experiment and the mechanisms underlying the participants' seemingly inexplicable human behavior.

Auditioning re-enactors for his performance, Dickinson looked for professional performers whose passion and conviction about the project matched his own. Gaskin observed that Dickinson's briefing notes were like a sermon in which the artist impressed upon the actors how the person they were playing would have spoken and acted. He appeared to inhabit Milgram's role. "Dickinson inhabits the methodologies of his subject, scrutinizing them in painful detail and, in so doing . . . 'becomes' them," she noted.[7] There was a running joke at the gallery that it was just as well Dickinson made a career of art since, judging by the success with which he elicited obedience from the cast, he would have made a good cult leader. It was no coincidence that Dickinson's previous gallery re-enactment focused on a real-life cult leader, Jim Jones. The director was fascinated by the nature of belief; this was one of the key working ideas of *The Milgram Re-enactment*.

Dickinson positioned his audience behind the mock laboratory's surveillance window. This was the same position from which Milgram and his associates watched the drama unfold. (Milgram estimated he watched approximately one-third of the more than 800 experimental sessions.) Audience members were asked not to leave the performance space for the duration—four hours in total. Not everyone complied—no surprise there! One reviewer lasted two hours, reporting them as among the longest two hours of her life. This sense of time weighing heavily was intentional. Dickinson aimed to create a situation in which the audience was trapped in front of the shock machine and forced to become voyeurs.

The Milgram Re-enactment is a compelling, if austere, production. When it was first presented, few researchers had spent time working with materials from the Stanley Milgram Papers archive. As the files have been subjected to increased scrutiny, it has become clear that the nonprofessional actors for this production frequently departed from the script. After rehearsing and staging his re-enactments, Dickinson concluded that "the experiment sets up a drama that like some of Beckett's plays, gains gravity and resonance through repetition."[8] As one watches Dickinson's re-enactment, the image that comes to mind is a succession of people blind to the consequences of their actions.

IMPROVISED RE-ENACTMENT

I completed my own feature documentary about Milgram's "Obedience to Authority" experiments, *Shock Room*, in 2015.[9] The project had been in development for approximately seven years. Initially, I planned an essay film focused on those participants who resisted. Imagine black-and-white film, drive-by footage of the streets of New Haven and Bridgeport, crime scene re-enactments, a tough-talking narrator (preferably a woman), and a jazz score. In story terms, I saw the project as following in the footsteps of Cesare Zavattini's *inchestia*, or film inquiry. One of the architects of neorealism, screenwriter and journalist Zavattini proposed the *inchestia* as a new form of nonfiction.[10] Re-enactments were critical, allowing audiences some distance from events to enable seeing them with fresh eyes.

On the research trail, I traveled to New York to see Alexandra Milgram, who had managed her husband's archive since his death in 1981. In New Haven, I tracked down several of Milgram's original participants who had publicly identified themselves as disobedient subjects. They were now in their nineties, and if I was going to interview them, time was of the essence. Awarded script development funds to research and write a feature documentary, I produced several treatments. The first iteration of the project was called "The Man Who Said No." It was inspired by the balding businessman at the end of Milgram's documentary who refuses to continue. Told by the Experimenter that he has no choice but to inflict electric shocks, the businessman crosses his arms and says, "Oh, I have plenty of choices" (figure 7.1). At campus screenings of Milgram's film during the Vietnam War, students cheered him. Did he ever know that? Did he ever even see the film in which he took one of the leading roles?

At times, I felt like a detective in my own noir movie—poring over files as the clock edged toward midnight, my desk lamp casting shadows on the wall.

Figure 7.1. *Obedience*, Stanley Milgram, 1965.

Waking in the night, I would picture the finding aid to the Stanley Milgram
Papers and mentally scroll through it. How could I identify the balding businessman—a folk hero to some? Was there a clue I had missed somewhere?
Scrawled on a record I thought was his, I found a handwritten comment: "a mean
bastard." Surely that could not be true?

I dipped into my files to look at the endless documents generated: script drafts,
funding proposals, budgets, and lists of interested parties who signed up for
meetings. I was in development hell, the on-off (but mostly off) process that
many writers and producers endure as they attempt to obtain financing for films.
Typically, it involves participating in a market where you pitch your project to
interested broadcasters and distributors in a series of brief meetings. The aim is
to piece together a jigsaw of presales and distribution guarantees. Should you
be selected to participate—and competition is fierce—attending pitch school in
advance is mandatory. You are coached through a standardized elevator spiel
for your project until, gradually, anything that may be distinctive about it has
been eroded.

The largest obstacle to funding *The Man Who Said No* was that most commissioning editors believed Milgram's "Obedience to Authority" studies were
"gold standard." Interesting as this new emphasis on resistance may be, science
unit colleagues told them the research did not bear it out. Their source?

Milgram's book *Obedience to Authority*, published in 1974. I sent them copies of just-published psychology papers. We went around in circles. My patience wore thin. My sense of humor went missing in action. I canceled a follow-up meeting with an interested commissioning editor when he asked me whether our re-enactments could be performed ethically. "Yes," I assured him. He appeared disappointed. "It would be a lot more fun if people really did get hurt," he said.

Shifting direction, I financed the film via research grants instead. We would have a smaller budget but more creative and intellectual freedom. Ultimately, I restaged selected versions of Milgram's drama in a studio with actors using an immersive realism performance method I had developed for a pilot. In 2012, I filmed *Random 8* based on the "Unjust Authority Encounter" devised by sociologist William Gamson, who pioneered simulations of the kind in which I had participated as a student.[11] In an early challenge to Milgram's "Obedience to Authority" experiments, Gamson and his colleagues devised a study in which people agreed to participate in market research groups at a local Holiday Inn. They were asked to undertake a series of unjust requests made by an authority figure. I restaged the "Unjust Authority Encounter" with improvising actors.[12]

On *Shock Room*, we built a contemporary version of Milgram's laboratory set, complete with a shock machine. I drew on extensive archival research that I had undertaken in the Milgram Archives for much of the detail. Additionally, social psychology collaborators Alex Haslam and Steve Reicher consulted throughout a lengthy development process. Our audiences followed nine fictional characters through dramatizations. They were men and women of different ages and different cultural and socioeconomic backgrounds. Fascinating as they are to watch, it is easy to dismiss the participants in Milgram's 1965 film as historical figures from another era. I wanted to bring the "Obedience to Authority" experiments alive for contemporary audiences. I cast actors with experience in theater, as well as skilled film actors capable of sustaining long, structured improvisations. The actors simply knew they would be playing a volunteer in a psychology experiment and could bail out at any time. As on *Random 8*, I sketched the characters in collaboration with the individual actors to ensure a representative mix of contemporary citizens. Then, the actors conducted further research to bring their invented characters to life. My brief to cast members was that they were responsible for responding in the scenario moment by moment as their character (figures 7.2 and 7.3). When the cinematographer and I first discussed the film, we decided it was crucial to capture each character's session as a complete entity. We needed many cameras to cover the interpersonal dynamics. We shot using three main cameras behind a two-way mirror and several micro-cameras built into the laboratory's physical space.

On set, it immediately became apparent that the material was dramatic. It was like watching filmed live theater, each actor's "first take" running for up to twenty minutes and appearing on multiple monitors. Our psychology advisers,

Figure 7.2. *Shock Room*, Charlie Productions, 2015.

Figure 7.3. *Shock Room*, Charlie Productions, 2015.

Alex Haslam and Steve Reicher, observed from a studio control room. I later shot interviews with them, drawing on their interpretations of the dynamics of obedience and resistance. There was always tension regarding whether the re-enactments were drama or experiments. For me, they were 100 percent drama. We worked in a studio where the film crew and equipment were clearly visible. The actors were directed. The performance style and long takes contributed to a sense of hyperrealism. That same tension continued to play out in screenings. Audiences composed of psychologists claimed *Shock Room*'s dramatizations as experiments. Film festival audiences burst out laughing at the notion of basing statistics on the behavior of actors playing fictional characters. The material may have *looked* real, but that was due to what has been termed cinema's "reality effect."[13] As a medium, film can create an impression of authenticity—an effect that can be deliberately accentuated by aesthetic choices. Critic Hanna Schenkel wrote, "Like Milgram, Millard allows the footage of her experiment to unroll on screen; devoid of musical accompaniment or commentary, it gives the impression of being a scientific study's indexical footage."[14] Our improvised re-enactments of different versions of the experiment were interspersed with contextual information about Milgram's work and the ways in which it had been challenged, conveyed via animation, text on screen, and narration.

Many of the ways re-enactment in documentary is categorized emphasize the historical veracity and its audiovisual markers. Bill Nichols proposed the following major types of documentary re-enactment: historically realist, historically specific, realist and historically specific, stylized, Brechtian distanced, and ironic.[15] To this list, I would add improvised re-enactment, whose hallmarks include long takes and performances that appear to unfold in real time. *Shock Room* provides one example. But writing about one's own work is difficult—it always seems best to discuss aspirations rather than outcomes. Hence, I will give the last word to Schenkel: "*Shock Room* makes clear that it is one piece of a much larger puzzle, open to engagement and criticism."[16]

THE BIOGRAPHICAL FILM

I was reluctant to watch *Experimenter* until I had completed my own film. An independent feature film, written and directed by Michael Almereyda, *Experimenter* aimed to focus public attention on Milgram's life and body of work.[17] Eventually, I sat down to view it. To all intents and purposes, the film is an authorized biopic that takes an inventive approach to tell the story of its subject's life (figure 7.4). After reading transcripts of experimental sessions, Almereyda became fascinated with the experimental psychologist. He struck a deal with Alexandra Milgram, and she shared her memories and assigned him the rights to depict her late husband's life on film. One of the challenges of the material was that the film's key subject was far from a typical leading man. As Almereyda commented, "Milgram is very much a guy whose life was spent reading, writing, and thinking, so his experiments become the movie's essential action—a primary way Milgram interacts with people, even as he observes them from a distance."[18] Almereyda also felt that the controversy surrounding the ethics of the "Obedience to Authority" studies may have overshadowed Milgram's later experiments.

Despite strong support from major independent festivals, including Sundance, *Experimenter* took eight years to reach the screen. The final budget was considerably less than initially envisaged. Almereyda, who had worked across

Figure 7.4. *Experimenter*, Magnolia Home Entertainment, 2015.

both drama and documentary, made a virtue out of necessity, drawing on cinematic devices such as sets and rear projection to shoot *Experimenter* in only twenty days. *Experimenter* re-created Milgram's laboratory in a set and shot several key scenes on location at Yale University. The film's production designer, Deana Sidney, commented that "colour was very important to us all and we had the film move through an ever-brightening world."[19] The film's palette was initially based on a color photograph of the original laboratory that, over time, had skewed to a yellowish green. At the last minute, the director decided to switch from this alienating color to a range of more soothing blue-greens. The overall effect is that of a heightened, slightly theatrical world.

Peter Sarsgaard, who played Milgram, has discussed the challenges of the role. Describing the character as "phlegmatic" and "dispassionate," he noted that these were unusual qualities for an actor to be asked to portray. Conceptualizations of individual temperament like these go back to the ancient Greek typology developed by Hippocrates (fourth century B.C.E.) and Galen (second century B.C.E.). The well-known types of temperament, based on humors or bodily types, were sanguine, choleric, melancholic, and phlegmatic.[20] Phlegmatic was considered calm, unresponsive, and cool. In constructing his performance, Sarsgaard also took clues from Milgram's appearances in a series of short educational documentaries in the 1970s. The actor observed that the psychologist looked uncomfortable in his own skin, and he had a difficult relationship with the camera.[21] In one of the educational documentaries in which he appeared, Milgram walked down the street in a corduroy jacket talking to the camera. He had a glass of wine that he pretended to drink as he did so. Unsurprisingly, the result was far from relaxed. After watching Milgram's filmed media appearances, Sarsgaard described his on-camera persona as having a forced casual quality. This aspect did not make him an entirely sympathetic character to play.

To allow us to get under the skin of its subject, *Experimenter* directly addresses the camera. As Milgram, Sarsgaard frequently turns and voices his thoughts to the audience as events occur around him. This method is often used to foster intimacy with the audience; in this case, however, Milgram is predominantly shown sharing musings on his work. Sarsgaard's carefully calibrated performance suggests an open-minded man with a sense of curiosity, yet someone who was never off duty. He watches from behind the two-way mirror in his laboratory. Watches the people around him on the streets. Watches—well, you get the picture. It is unsurprising that Milgram aspired to direct more films. He was far more comfortable in the role of writer and director, observing from behind the scenes, than as an on-screen personality.

I recall once finding a cartridge of Super 8 film shot by Milgram among the Stanley Milgram Papers at Yale University. Despite Milgram's strong interest in lens-based media, I found little actual film or photographic material in this archive. The Super 8 film was a cause for excitement. The box was labeled "Circle Film." Did it document a small group discussion? Would it shed any light on Milgram's thought processes? After receiving permission to have the material digitized, I watched the resulting several minutes of footage. A small group of people stand in a circle on a city street, gazing up at the sky. Passersby soon stop and join them. What is everyone looking at? The unremarkable footage provided a glimpse of the "social proof" demonstration that Milgram conducted with students from City University of New York in the 1970s. The group gathered on the pavement and looked toward the sky. It was not long before people passing by joined them.

Experimenter's closing scene re-creates the demonstration. Alexandra Milgram, then in her eighties, stands on a New York City street. She looks up to the sky. The scene is moving—especially after Winona Ryder's portrayal of her as a vibrant younger woman deeply involved with her husband's career. My initial reluctance to watch *Experimenter* was unfounded. It is a thoughtful and strikingly visualized film that pushes beyond the standard biopic or life story of a great man. But, however inventive and well crafted it is as an authorized account of Milgram's life, *Experimenter* still tells a familiar story about the "Obedience to Authority" experiments.

VERBATIM

Several years after *Shock Room*, I remained unable to let the material go. I found myself making a short verbatim film, *Experiment 20*, in collaboration with psychologist Stephen Gibson. Drawing on rhetorical analysis as a method, Gibson had long worked with audio recordings and transcripts from the Stanley Milgram

Papers, exploring issues of resistance and refusal to cooperate.[22] Produced for online contexts, *Experiment 20* dramatized the transcripts of three of the women in Milgram's experiments, encompassing both their sessions at the shock machine and their debriefs.[23] Something of an afterthought, Milgram's "Women as Subjects" version of his experiment was run very late in the series of experiments. The women, mainly recruited via their husbands, included nurses, medical technicians, clerks, housekeepers, and housewives. Milgram reported that the results for women were identical to those for men, although, overall, women appeared to experience more internal conflict than men. Milgram's cursory observation regarding women participants did not always seem borne out by the transcripts.

Experiment 20 combined "verbatim performance" techniques with aspects of film noir to create a shadow world of darkness and ambiguity. The actors channeled individual characters, creating performances while listening to the original participants' actual recorded voices via concealed earpieces. We aimed to tell the story in the words of the women, re-creating every pause, hesitation, nervous laugh, and sigh. In the version told by the data, the "Obedience to Authority" story was black-and-white. Participants were coded "1" for "obedient" or "2" for "disobedient." There were no shades of gray, no spaces in between. However, listening to the audiotapes, we could hear a different story. These three women resisted the Experimenter—albeit in markedly different ways—displaying everything from anger and exasperation to calm determination.

A twenty-six-year-old unemployed nurse said that she had participated in many psychology experiments in New Haven. After refusing to continue at 315 volts, she was classified as "disobedient." The young nurse had a keen interest in psychology and was remarkably successful at eliciting information from the Experimenter during her debrief, expressing great interest in the research and asking a series of well-informed questions. At times, it appeared that she was the one actually running the debrief. The Experimenter revealed to her that male participants were not told that the shocks received by the Victim were not real. Far from panicking, many women demanded a great deal more information than their male counterparts in debriefs and interviews.

Given the pseudonym "Gretchen Brandt," another young woman was presented as one of the brief case studies in Stanley Milgram's *Obedience to Authority*. The psychologist described her as "an attractive 31-year-old medical technician who works at the University Medical School."[24] She had emigrated from Germany five years prior and spoke with a definite German accent. Classified as "disobedient," Brandt was resolute throughout her session. At the point where she was required to administer what she believed to be a shock of 210 volts, Brandt turned to the Experimenter and said, "Well, I'm sorry, I don't think we should continue." According to Milgram, this is what he had hoped for from all the participants—a straightforward and courteous refusal to go on.[25]

Listening to the audiotapes and workshopping them with the actors, it was apparent that the medical technician did not just straightforwardly refuse but instead put forward a range of arguments to justify her decision to discontinue. Was the learner (i.e., the Victim) willing to keep going? If so, Brandt said she too would continue. Reminding the Experimenter that the learner had a heart condition, Brandt insisted that she was personally responsible for any harm to him. Implicit in her statement was that the Experimenter was also responsible for his actions. Brandt stated that she would not like to be in his position. As she reminded the Experimenter, "We came here of our free will." So much for simply being calm and resolute under pressure. In fact, Brandt constantly generated new arguments and strategies as she tried to persuade the Experimenter of her point of view and prevent a man from being harmed.

As theater director Robin Soans noted, "Verbatim documentary provides settings in which otherwise lost voices can be amplified."[26] It encourages us to listen carefully to people, including those not necessarily from our own tribes. Performance and film can help us envisage the gestures and movements of social actors who are absent from the historical record, such as the women participants. As audience members, we can stand in for the interviewer or become witnesses. In the end, one older female participant reluctantly concedes. She has repeatedly told the Experimenter that she was not nervous but "good and mad"—and completely ignored. Their exchange is protracted. "Oh, put it there, I suppose," she says, arbitrarily marking a spot on his form and sighing. "Thanks," says the Experimenter. He finally has his data. However, the data does not tell the story of their encounter.

LIVE CINEMA

A hierarchy that attributes a seriousness of purpose and method to science while denying the same to the creative arts has often dismissed Milgram's "Obedience to Authority" as "just theater." As the Stanley Milgram Papers have opened up, the degree to which the experiments relied on design and dramaturgy has become even more apparent. Consequently, it has now become commonplace to describe Milgram's experiments as "beautifully constructed drama." Such statements are used to support the "Obedience to Authority" studies as compelling science. In applying for additional research funding to make a documentary, Milgram argued that it was imperative to document his experimental procedure. He intended that other psychologists would be able to replicate the "Obedience to Authority" studies. However, the subsequent controversy regarding their ethics meant that the experiments could not easily be repeated. The few recent attempts by psychologists to do so have involved strategies such as participants being asked to inflict shocks up to 150 volts, rather than the 450 volts of Milgram's original version.[27] Some so-called scientific reprisals, such as *The*

Game of Death, broadcast in France, are best viewed as entertainment. This particular case is a hybrid form of reality television and game show in which the participation of a psychologist is simply part of the theater.

Live cinema is a relatively new contemporary form—one to which Milgram's *Obedience: A Drama* would be well suited. Katie Mitchell is one of the key founders and practitioners of this form that fuses elements of theater and film. Mitchell has described recorded cinema as limited "because it is not really happening." By contrast, live cinema involves the film being remade and projected in each performance. Adapting Virginia Woolf's novel *The Waves*, Mitchell's production combined action onstage with visible roving cameras and live and recorded sound. The result was projected above the stage, with camera coverage enabling close observation of minute shifts in behavior. Moreover, according to performance theorist Adam Ledger, the form foregrounds the construction of the version the audience is watching. "Mitchell emphasises the actuality of sometimes frenetic on-stage filmmaking, which subsequently renders the highly crafted, often consciously aestheticized realism of the film," observed Ledger.[28]

Inevitably, just as the society around us changes, art forms continuously shift and develop. The productions I have discussed stage "Obedience to Authority" as a drama exploring a range of themes and key ideas—the nature of belief (*The Milgram Re-enactment*), television as an authority figure (*Game of Death*), resistance and human agency (*Shock Room*), the perspectives of women participants (*Experiment 20*), and the intellectual biography of Stanley Milgram (*Experimenter*). Their chosen genres span the art gallery re-enactment, reality television, essay film, verbatim documentary, and biopic or biographical film. After all, genres are not fixed story patterns. They continually reinvent themselves, branching or merging and hybridizing.

CHAPTER 8

"I Was the SYSTEM"

We rewrite our lives as if they were stories. We redraft those stories as if they were movies. Novelist Patrick Modiano, whose atmospheric tales are infused with the search for lost people, lost places, and lost light, recalled his own life as "a simple black-and-white film of facts and deeds."[1] Philip Zimbardo, a self-confessed movie tragic, rewrote his own life on a grander scale. The psychologist's love affair with cinema began when his parents took him to see *Gone with the Wind* when he was a small boy. The Technicolor melodrama, with its heightened hues and emotions, made a strong impression. The movies that stuck with him most over the years explored three themes: evil, heroism, and hedonism.[2] Zimbardo became an avid filmgoer; indeed, he credited cinema with inspiring his work as a psychologist.

Zimbardo's preferred template for his own life story was the redemption narrative—the American version. Given the controversy around his dual role as experimenter and authority figure who sanctioned prisoner abuse, it was not initially the most promising material. There was a complex authorial process. Zimbardo was sixty-nine years old when he began consulting on the script for *The Stanford Prison Experiment* (the 2015 film) in 2002. Written by Tim Talbot and produced by Christopher McQuarrie, this iteration of the project followed several other attempts to adapt the role play to the big screen.[3] The psychologist would not sign any deal without an assurance that the resulting film would reflect what had really happened at Stanford—that is, what had really happened according to Philip Zimbardo.

"I was the SYSTEM," reads a handwritten note on the cover of a draft of *The Stanford Prison Experiment* screenplay.[4] Deposited in the Philip Zimbardo Papers at Stanford University is a draft dated 2006. Zimbardo's notes, which are mostly scrawled on its title page, evidence the input of a college professor alongside the insights of a would-be dramatist. Typos and poor grammar are

circled. Unsubstantiated assertions about matters, such as the length of the simulation or the presence of particular personnel at any given time, are corrected.
Selected lines are rewarded with "interesting." I can almost imagine Zimbardo's red pen hovering over the text. His brief, cryptic jottings offer some clues as
to the psychologist's thoughts and suggestions on the draft. I wonder if that is
why he chose to deposit this version in the archive—to clarify his contribution?
I can only imagine it would be a confronting process to subject your life's work
to scrutiny by others, examining your motivations and most significant relationships. As one reads Zimbardo's notes on the script, one aspect stands out.
He sought to align his account more closely with the redemption story template. Along the way, he borrowed from cinema and popular culture.

REDEMPTION STORIES

Narrative psychologist Dan McAdams proposes that well-functioning Americans most often see their lives as redemption stories. People typically craft stories of overcoming a series of obstacles to achieve success. McAdams traces the
redemptive life story pattern back to the New England Puritans. To become full
members of the church, adults were expected to give a satisfactory life narrative
about the development of their faith, after which members of the congregation
debated the value of each person's account.[5] Redemptive stories abound in television talk shows, cinema, the self-help shelves of bookshops, Christian sermons,
twelve-step programs, political rhetoric, novels, and more. We draw on all these
sources, plus family and community narratives, in crafting our own stories.
Script guru Robert McKee identifies the redemption plot as Hollywood's preferred story line. Such narratives, which hinge on the nuanced story of a central
character who changes from bad to good, dominate the Academy Award list of
winners, says McKee..[6] There is little complexity in McKee's narrative prescrip-
tion—it is aimed at attracting A-list actors.

Among Zimbardo's favorite films as he redrafted his life narrative were *Black
Orpheus*, "a thrilling narrative of evil versus good," and *The Most Dangerous Man
in America: Daniel Ellsberg and the Pentagon Papers*. The latter he found remarkable for its depiction of its central character's transformation "from agent of the
State Department to traitor."[7] Ellsberg's release of the Pentagon Papers contributed to ending the Vietnam War, and he was one of Zimbardo's personal heroes.
The film that seems to have made the greatest impact on the psychologist was
the prison movie *Cool Hand Luke* (1967), starring Paul Newman. It was a "les-
son in how corrupt systems dealt with individuals who refused to comply with
their rules."[8] Zimbardo particularly admired Newman's performance as the rebel
Luke—a man who would rather die than conform.

Feature films based on Zimbardo's prison simulation were in development
for several decades before finally reaching the big screen. *The Stanford Prison*

Experiment (2015) was reportedly the fourth or fifth iteration of the project.[9] At one stage, Leonardo DiCaprio was attached as one of the student volunteers in a film to be produced by Twentieth Century Fox. As is so often the case in the film industry, there was a personal connection—DiCaprio's father, who had been one of Zimbardo's students, was one of the project's producers. Following the critical and box office success of *Titanic*, it was hoped that the Hollywood star could help "pump up the gross." The writer of *Fight Club* was working on the script.[10] However, the project was canceled by Twentieth Century Fox when a competing version emerged.

Potential film adaptations attracted more than their share of legal disputes. *Das Experiment* (*The Experiment*) (2002), set in modern Germany, claimed to be based on a social experiment depicted in Mario Giordano's novel *Black Box*.[11] However, the film's story line was almost identical to that of Zimbardo's experiment. It changed the protagonist from the psychologist to an ex-journalist in search of a good story. Oliver Hirschbiegel, director of *Das Experiment*, looked to films about World War II for inspiration, specifically the submarine film *Das Boot*.[12] As Peter Rollins has observed, ships have proved popular settings for psychological dramas: "The dramatic potential of a ship with its confined space, placement within an un-survivable natural element, dependence on technology and confined characters is heightened when the ship becomes a submarine."[13] Like the popular submarine genre—if it can be called a genre—the Stanford Prison simulation was a drama of confinement. On completion, *Das Experiment* was promoted as a film about a failed psychological experiment. After Zimbardo and Stanford University sought legal advice, a statement claiming that the film was inspired by the "Stanford Prison Experiment" run by Philip Zimbardo was removed from the film's credits.

When *Das Experiment* was released in the United States, two competing Hollywood projects were in development—*The Stanford Prison Experiment* (2015) and *The Experiment* (2010). Maverick Films had purchased the picture rights to the story from Zimbardo. Those rights included the story, characters, and the book that Zimbardo was yet to write, *The Lucifer Effect*.[14] *The Stanford Prison Experiment* stalled when a competitor pitched a rival project at the same market. Inferno declined an invitation to participate in *The Stanford Prison Experiment* and launched its own project, *The Experiment*. Consequently, Maverick sued—the company had been conned into revealing "in great detail their creative, business and other plans to produce, finance and market the film."[15] Next, Inferno countersued—it was making an English-language version of *Das Experiment*. The two companies finally reached a settlement, allowing *The Experiment* to enter production in 2008. A thriller, the movie starred Hollywood actor Adrian Brody in the lead role of the ex-journalist. *The Experiment* was predominantly seen as a by-the-numbers thriller, albeit with strong performances.

The Stanford Prison Experiment, with Zimbardo attached as a consultant, finally reached the big screen in 2015. Rather than the major Hollywood movie initially envisaged, it was an independent film with a low budget to match. Scriptwriter Tim Talbot aimed to cover all the major events of the six-day simulation.[16] The film was pitched as a chilling edge-of-your-seat thriller about the effects of imprisonment. Its closing credits read, "Based on *The Lucifer Effect*," *The Stanford Prison Experiment* follows the day-by-day structure initially established in Zimbardo's slide-tape presentation of 1971 and subsequently expanded on in *The Lucifer Effect*.

From the beginning, the official narrative of the "Stanford Prison Experiment" was written like a Hollywood film treatment—present tense and third person, as if we were watching the event unfold. Implicit was a narrative arc much like the standard Hollywood three-act drama, progressing through the setup, conflict, and resolution. In real life, of course, there existed messiness and confusion not captured by this particular story pattern. What did not change, though, were Zimbardo's conclusions, which are captured in the subtitle for his book, *How Good People Turn Evil*.

"Burton bragging about sleeping with best friend's wife," reads one of Zimbardo's notes on *The Stanford Prison Experiment* screenplay.[17] The three feature films based on Zimbardo's experiment produced to date (*Das Experiment*, *The Experiment*, and *The Stanford Prison Experiment*) have one key aspect in common: they were all ensemble films for predominantly male casts. They were all films—at least in part—about masculinity. Structurally, the protagonist and antagonist roles were shared by a group of actors. They formed part of a long line of movies featuring groups of men under pressure, from the submarine crew in *Das Boot* to the jury in *Twelve Angry Men* and the prison gang in *Cool Hand Luke*. Women make few appearances. Christina Maslach, Zimbardo's then fiancée, was a notable exception. The scene description of *The Stanford Prison Experiment* screenplay introduces the Christina character "as only a few years older than the boys, a freshly minted PhD and right hand to the man wrapping up his pitch (Zimbardo)."[18] From the story's beginning to end, Maslach acts as Zimbardo's conscience, voicing concerns about the ethics of the simulation.

The Bechdel test, devised by artist and graphic novelist Alison Bechdel, aims to determine whether women in a given film are fully developed characters or primarily plot devices to support the stories of male characters. The test comprises three questions. First, are there more than three named female characters? Second, do two female characters have a conversation with each other at any point? Third, is that conversation about anything other than a male character? To pass the Bechdel test, the answer to all three questions for any given film must be an unequivocal yes. Would any of the films inspired by social psychology's key experiments pass? No.

By their very nature, adaptations update stories for new audiences and contexts. As Arthur Frank argued in his socio-narratology of stories, "If, according to Heraclitus's maxim, a person can never step into the same river twice, so also the same story is never told twice."[19] Zimbardo's 1971 prison role play was based on a simulation designed by his students that same year. The latter included both men and women. The psychologist chose to make his version all male. Why make the same decision three decades later?

Women are radically underrepresented in the Hollywood film industry. Overall, the percentage of female speaking roles in Hollywood has remained virtually the same since the 1940s. That statistic hovers around 25 to 30 percent. Only 15 percent of lead roles are taken by women, and women are paid significantly less than their male counterparts. Behind the camera, men vastly outnumber women in key roles, including screenwriter, director, cinematographer, composer, and executive producer.[20] The same story plays out across the globe. Films with story lines and characters that appeal to men are far more likely to be produced.

"Not accurate" or "very accurate," Zimbardo noted on some scenes in Talbot's 2006 version of *The Stanford Prison Experiment* screenplay.[21] Both the psychology consultant and filmmakers emphasized the sense of authenticity common to realistic genres such as the prison film. However, this could be taken too far. Director Kyle Alvarez saw the confined space and monotony of the material as the shoot's central limitations. "Every scene is basically a prisoner gets abused and locked up. Next scene. A prisoner gets abused and locked up. It's the same scene over and over again," said Alvarez.[22] His brief to his actors was this: "You are a professional role player portraying an amateur role player. Just the kind of person likely to lose control."[23] The direction implied that performers should be looking for opportunities to do just that—lose control—as they plotted character journeys.

After I watched *The Stanford Prison Experiment*, one key scene lodged itself in my memory. It is the kind of private rehearsal of public behavior that Erving Goffman described as backstage performance.[24] Three student guards change into their uniforms before going on shift. In this setting, their behavior is primarily aimed at impressing their peers. Slightly giddy with their newly acquired power, the guards check their uniforms in a mirror. One of them, Eschelman, faces the mirror. Brandishing his baton, he admires his new look. He then adds the finishing touch—his own mirrored sunglasses. Addressing his reflection, Eschelman quotes the warden in *Cool Hand Luke*: "Now I can be a nice guy . . . or I can be a real mean sun'bitch. It's all up to you."[25]

Zimbardo insisted that the original "Stanford Prison Experiment" participant's reference to the tough warden character in *Cool Hand Luke* (played by Strother Martin) was spontaneous. However, that claim has been disputed, and the evidence suggests otherwise.[26] The mirrored sunglasses worn by student guards make numerous appearances in *The Lucifer Effect* and Zimbardo's media interviews. The psychologist recalled how impressed he was by a police officer's sunglasses: "He put on his silver reflecting glasses, the kind the guard wore in the movie *Cool Hand Luke*, the kind that prevents anyone from seeing your eyes."[27] Casting himself as the prison superintendent in his experiment, Zimbardo put on his own mirrored sunglasses but could never imagine himself as a jailer. Zimbardo confessed, "I could imagine myself as a Paul Newman kind of wisely resistant prisoner, as portrayed in . . . *Cool Hand Luke*."[28] The kid who grew up in the Bronx, loved the movies, and saw himself as a liberal reformer identified with the cool antiauthority figure.

SEEING THE LIGHT

Throughout *The Stanford Prison Experiment*, Zimbardo is shown in an observation room watching events on video as they unfold. The psychologist dismisses others' serious concerns and ignores opportunities to intervene—the experiment must continue at all costs. Billy Crudup's portrait of Zimbardo is less than flattering. "The psychology professor comes across as a borderline-sadistic scholar who held minimal regard for the harm his research might inflict on his subjects," one reviewer wrote.[29]

The Stanford Prison Experiment is a film about seeing. However, redemption movies are always about seeing. According to Dan McAdams, six kinds of language are used in redemption stories in contemporary American culture: atonement, emancipation, upward mobility, recovery, enlightenment, and development. The language usually varies according to the context. Stories of enlightenment and insight, associated with the fields of education and science, involve a shift from ignorance to knowledge.[30] Working back and forth across his book, media appearances, and consulting on screenplay drafts, Zimbardo rewrites his own life narrative as a redemptive story of enlightenment. A highly trained and experienced psychologist becomes so immersed in an abusive situation that he is unable to recognize his own role in it. Finally, with the help of a good woman—well, Zimbardo did have some help from Hollywood to rewrite his life story—he is able to see.

In "Notes on Seeing," novelist and essayist Siri Hustvedt states that "'I see' can also mean 'I understand.'"[31] In a Christian parable, Jesus miraculously restored the sight of a blind beggar, Lazarus. The latter became a believer, proclaiming, "Once I was blind, now I see." "Add *Amazing Grace* scene," Zimbardo scrawled on the draft screenplay.[32] In the movie, this was a brief incident in which the guards forced prisoners to sing the hymn. Authoring his own narrative in both *The Lucifer Effect* and *The Stanford Prison Experiment* (as much as a rights holder and psychology consultant can influence the story line), Zimbardo presented himself as the man who finally sees and is, thus, reborn. To do so, he had to paint his behavior in an even harsher light—darkness always precedes seeing the light.

Another version of the American redemption narrative focuses on people who give up crime, drugs, or alcohol. Criminologist Shadd Maruna, who has interviewed and conducted fieldwork with many such individuals, concluded that fashioning a logical, believable, and respectable story of change is central to this process. A reform story salvages a good self from the past and integrates it into a productive future. Along the way, individuals play a series of personae, beginning with the victim and progressing through the roles of delinquent, outlaw, and fortunate one. Eventually, the narrator finds goals involving generativity (or contributing to future generations) and becomes a streetwise savior. The reforming person often must reach back deep into the past to find the self who needs reforming to construct such a story successfully.[33] Aspects of this story are borrowed from cinema as the narrator makes sense of their own life.

The life story of reformed prisoner Carlo Prescott may well have lent itself to such treatment. Prescott co-taught with Zimbardo early in his career and advised on both the student prison simulation and the Stanford Prison simulation. Months later, he presented evidence in the form of his own redemption story to a congressional committee examining prison reform. This account began with his arrest and imprisonment at thirteen years of age after stealing a sandwich from a food truck.[34] A crime resulting from poverty and hunger jump-starts the first chapter of his reform story.

"Make Christina the hero," reads one of Zimbardo's notes on Talbot's early draft.[35] Seeing a group of mock prisoners moved with paper bags over their heads as guards shouted at them shocked the young psychologist. Philip Zimbardo's indifference to this sight shocked her yet further. "I was angry and frightened and in tears," reported the real-life Christina Maslach. "I said something like, 'what you are doing to those boys is a terrible thing!'"[36] As a young woman, Maslach challenged an authority figure and forced him to see that he was complicit in prisoner abuse. Ultimately, her actions led him to abandon the simulation. According to Zimbardo, Maslach did not consider herself a hero because, unlike a whistleblower, she did not have to make a case to higher authorities. Nevertheless, Zimbardo changed his behavior due to Maslach's intervention.[37]

A quick search of Google Books tells me that Zimbardo uses the word *hero* no fewer than forty-four times in *The Lucifer Effect*. The lengthy discussion of Maslach's behavior in his book and the events as depicted in the screenplay are not entirely in sync, in part due to the complexity of the issues under discussion. Was Maslach's behavior simply an emotional outburst? (Her term, not his.) An incidence of "behavioral disobedience" not followed up by meaningful action such as a report to authorities? Or an act of bravery in the public interest? The feature film drama is not best suited to the exploration of such concepts; inevitably, due to the limitations of time and budget, some real-life events are expanded while others are compressed or omitted. Questioning notions of heroism was not a key theme of *The Stanford Prison Experiment*. However, making Christina Maslach the hero was important to Zimbardo. It was one of the plot points on which his own life story hinged. He was saved from himself, and his willingness to listen cemented a relationship that was then in its early stages.

Film historian Sam Girgus credits Hollywood with creating a uniquely American cinema of redemption: "In the classic American version of the cinema, the hero undergoes a crisis of identity, culminating in a transforming or conversion experience."[38] A body of American film work from the 1930s to 1960s, spanning genres including dramas, historical narratives, westerns, and love stories, brought a sense of triumph to screen stories of redemption.

By his account, one late chapter in Zimbardo's life review was dedicated to a role he termed "Prosecutor." Seeing his readers as a jury, Zimbardo aimed to expose them to a background of the crimes of the top brass in the U.S. military and the George W. Bush administration. These men and women were responsible for creating the institutional conditions that allowed prisoner abuse and torture to flourish. Zimbardo was at pains to highlight that, as surely as night follows day, "bad situations" created "bad apples" created "bad behaviors." The same chain reaction occurred even among good people. Crucially, this sidesteps the criticism Zimbardo has attracted for repeatedly appearing as a witness for the defense in the trials of those who have abused their charges. As even the most casual viewer of courtroom dramas knows, witness for the defense and witness for the prosecution are fundamentally different roles.

According to the director of *The Stanford Prison Experiment*, Zimbardo was someone who ultimately took ownership of his actions. In preparation for the shoot, the director and the actor Billy Crudup, who played Zimbardo, talked about "what it meant to get unwittingly wrapped up in something that becomes larger than you and the ambition of the man."[39] This suggests a cautionary tale rather than the redemption story its central character was penning in real life. Ultimately, *The Stanford Prison Experiment* was not Zimbardo's story to tell. It had escaped the oversight of its instigator and now belonged to the community.

A new chapter in Zimbardo's redemption story was the establishment of the Heroic Imagination Project, which ran training programs and produced short documentaries for online viewing. At the core of the initiative was the notion that we should all be trained to be everyday heroes. Judging by his long list of media appearances, Zimbardo has kept telling this story on current affairs and chat shows. According to Peter Brooks (the literature professor, not the theater director), the practice of confession, introduced into the Christian church in the thirteenth century, signaled the emergence of a narrative self in Western culture. Providing an account of a transgression to an accepting audience became a form of self-expression.[40] Memoirs, autobiographies, television talk shows, reality television, social media, and podcasts are just some of the current channels for confession. The accepting audience can be a priest, friend, therapist, police, jury, television viewers, or voters in an election.[41]

Here is one last script note from Philip Zimbardo: "Add my craziness at trying to get prisoners transferred to Old City Gaol."[42] By his own admission, the experimenter had lost all sense of the boundaries between role play and reality. But, of course, this is meant to justify the "reality" of the simulation. A 1971 U.S. Congress committee on prisons was impressed with Zimbardo's account of his experiment and his suggestions for reform.[43] However, not everyone was impressed with the notion that his prison was the real deal.

CHAPTER 9

Shifting the Story

It is a wintry Saturday afternoon in London. My partner and I wait in the foyer of Battersea Arts Centre. We have been summoned for jury duty. To be more accurate, we have purchased tickets to *The Justice Syndicate*, an interactive theater production and collaboration across performance and social psychology.[1] One of the project's artistic directors will meet the twelve audience members who make up today's jury. I glance around the foyer. Parents help young children in and out of coats and scarves. In the café, steam rises from an espresso machine. People cup their hands around mugs of hot drinks. The conversation is buzzing. Are any of those people our fellow jurists?

The ramshackle building, patches of peeling paint, and the hustle and bustle transport me back to youthful stints as a community arts activist. I feel right at home—this place has form when it comes to art and ideas. It was here that Bertrand Russell first read his essay "Why I Am Not a Christian" nearly a century ago. Once the Battersea Town Hall, the building took on a new life as a community arts venue in the 1970s. It now operates as a performance space with a "scratch" philosophy; that is, new productions are presented at various stages of their evolution, with audience responses playing a role in the development process. The works tested here can be large or small, and they typically combine art forms—live performance, animation, documentary, video games, music, and more. In the early decades of the twenty-first century, as in early cinema, mixes of recorded images and live performance are increasingly common.

How do you tell new stories when the old ones are broken? Since social psychology's foundation experiments were first staged, a wealth of new evidence has emerged. The bystander effect, for example, needs a rewrite. It looks like more of us are Good Samaritans rather than Bad Samaritans. Data gleaned from surveillance footage of streets at night—and, in some case, redacted police files—suggests that most people work together to intervene when they see someone hurt in public. (However, this is not always done successfully.)[2] The new evidence on bystander behavior is robust although, of course, it is also partial and incomplete. Surveillance footage captured by local authorities has blind spots, angles that the cameras do not cover—not to mention outages or equipment on the blink. To the frustration of many psychologists, it is difficult to gain much traction for new perspectives. I share that frustration. The court of public opinion shifts slowly. Some narratives are too successfully embedded in communities. This is perhaps because we always hear stories against the backdrop of other stories—fictional or real.

Sampling recent online news accounts of bystander events, I felt as if I was back in the 1960s. Take the following story. In Oceanside, New York, a group of high school students gathered outside a pizza place. A fight between two male students was planned. A dispute over a girl was the alleged reason for involvement. Events quickly spun out of control—one of the boys had a knife—and a fifteen-year-old boy died at the scene. Police and news estimates of the numbers of people who watched and filmed quickly escalated. Not one person stepped in to help during the brutal assault, a local police detective told a press conference: "They would rather video this event. They videoed his death instead of helping him."[3] Reportedly, this was the bystander effect in action. Here we go again, I thought. Old stories have force because they appear in so many different versions, suggested Francesca Polletta.[4] Their very diversity gives them the feel of common sense. This time, however, the official narrative was soon corrected.[5] Phone call logs recorded that many people did try to help.

As my investigation came to a close, I found myself drawn increasingly to legal scholars' work on stories. I had set out to shed light on new evidence, gleaned from archives, regarding the better side of human nature—particularly audiovisual evidence, some of which I had produced myself. However, one lifetime would not be long enough to make my way through all the relevant archives. It was time to cut to the chase. Work at the cusp of law, sociology, and social psychology that interested me concerned how individuals and groups constructed stories and, in particular, how narrative patterns borrowed from film and television informed what happened in real courtrooms.

Back in South London, Dan Barnard, one of the two artistic directors of *The Justice Syndicate*, arrives. Those of us attending this afternoon's performance step forward. I was not a fan of audience participation theater. It was something I associated with events such as the following: members of an experimental performance company calling out randomly chosen individual audience members, demanding they strip publicly while the crowd piled on the social pressure—no doubt to save themselves from being called on to do the same—or audience members being dragged onstage to dance with the cast and tell their life story to the world. No thanks! I went to theaters and performance spaces to observe, lose myself in depictions of other lives and worlds, and then reflect on my own.

Fortunately, *The Justice Syndicate* was not your usual audience participation show.

We follow Barnard up the stairs and enter a meeting room. Twelve chairs are placed around a table. Each place has an iPad, notepad, pen, and glass of water. Name cards indicate where "Juror 1" through "Juror 12" should sit. We are instructed to take a place. Across the room, computational artist Joe Allison and neuroscientist Kris De Meyer sit behind a desktop and mixing desk. Assistance is available for any technical problems; otherwise, the jury members are on their own. I gaze around the room. All but one of the members of our jury are women. Is that because this is a matinee performance? From here on, our instructions and evidence are presented via our individual preprogrammed tablets.

The research component of *The Justice Syndicate* had its roots in the work of Leon Festinger and his theory of cognitive dissonance.[6] According to the social scientist, individuals experience the world as a set of mental cognitions. Any behavior, attitude, or emotion can be a cognition—so, too, our perceptions of others and the physical world. Each person's set of cognitions and accompanying mental representations can fit together or not. In the latter case, people experience considerable psychological discomfort and seek to reduce this. Encountering information that challenges an integral part of our identity is particularly challenging. In turn, this leads to confirmation bias. One of the ways people can reduce the mental strain associated with cognitive dissonance is by doubling down on their initial attitude.[7]

Remember Festinger's false prophecy field experiment (discussed in chapter 1? The researchers began their study after reading the following headline: "Prophecy from Another Planet. Clarion Call to City: Flee That Flood. It'll Swamp Us on December 21, Outer Space Tells Suburbanite."[8] They contacted Mrs. Keech, leader of the fledgling social group, the Seekers, who had placed the advertisement. Could they observe meetings? She refused. Festinger and his colleagues decided to go undercover and attempt to join the group as believers. There were soon more participant observers than legitimate members gathering in Mrs. Keech's living room to prepare for the evacuation to an unknown planet.

Shortly after midnight on the appointed date, the mood was subdued. No visitors had appeared. Someone noticed that one clock still read 11:55 P.M. Relief. The outer space creatures were probably on their way. Soon, that clock struck midnight. There were still no visitors. One researcher's notes read: "There is no talking, no sound—people sit stock still, their faces seemingly frozen and expressionless."[9] At 4:00 A.M., people began searching for explanations. Mrs. Keech, the group's leader, was in tears. At 4:45 A.M., she received a message via automatic writing. The group's preparations demonstrated that they were a force of goodness and light—their actions had saved the entire world—their belief system was correct. There had simply been a change of plans. This was cognitive dissonance in action.[10]

According to social psychologist Joel Cooper, cognitive dissonance research owes its success to a two-punch strategy. *False Prophecy* was not an experiment, since there were no variables to control. Its findings—if that is what they were—were subject to considerable debate. Several years later, Festinger and his colleagues followed up with controlled laboratory experiments based on the perceptions of people assigned to perform boring tasks. In the decades since, many researchers have further tested and developed new theories of dissonance.[11] However, it was *False Prophecy*, with its dramatic story line and vivid images, that started the ball rolling.

"Studio One, Westinghouse Playhouse!" announces the enthusiastic narrator. I watch a black-and-white television program made in 1954.[12] At that time, television was still an event, one that sold, among other items, refrigerators and other appliances. Twelve jurors, all men, are seated in a courtroom. The camera stays on them as the judge gives his directions. They fidget uneasily. This is the fifty-minute television play, *Twelve Angry Men*, that preceded the film and stage versions. Dramatist Reginald Rose wrote his script shortly after serving a month on jury duty.[13] The event made a big impression; he realized that few people understood the interpersonal dynamics involved in a jury's deliberations. It was a good subject for a teleplay.

The Justice Syndicate belongs to a long tradition of theater and film about the law. Opportunities for dramatic tension, adversarial characters, and story reversals abound. Tele-plays closely resemble filmed theater. *Twelve Angry Men* went to air in 1954 against the backdrop of the Cold War. Only several months earlier, the hearings (or, should I say, interrogations?) of the House Committee on Un-American Activities were also broadcast live. Questions of innocence, guilt, and social pressure were in the very ether. *Twelve Angry Men* moved the action backstage to the jury room. In this setting, shifting allegiances and conflicts between jurors could be explored. Like the prison genre, the jury trial story was a good fit with social psychology. Both were ensemble dramas featuring (mostly) men under pressure.

According to *The Justice Syndicate* creative team, they drew on the jury trial format "to create a dramatic context for audience participation in the questioning of social issues."[14] One major point of departure was that their production involved only twelve participants with no audience members watching. Moreover, actors were confined to prerecorded testimonies. "We wanted to create an interactive experience in which a group of strangers can come together in person (rather than social media) and hold discussions that touch on what they value and care about in life," said the team.[15] The jury format was chosen because it is familiar and believable as a setting where a group of people come together to make a decision. There is also a long tradition of mock jury research aimed at shedding new light on the legal system's decision-making processes. Such research sits on the cusp of law and social psychology. Borrowing from the mock jury format, tests of individual and group decision-making were incorporated into the piece.

I first learned about mock jury trials at the Milgram Symposium at Yale Law School in 2013. The work of social psychologist Saul Kassin, a key inspiration for the Innocence Project, was particularly resonant. Based in the United States, the Innocence Project has successfully challenged many wrongful convictions involving false confessions.[16] Kassin saw parallels between the John Reid interrogation technique police have long used to elicit confessions and Milgram's "Obedience to Authority" paradigm. Devised by Chicago psychologist and former police officer John Reid in the 1950s, the interrogation technique placed people under enormous pressure to harm themselves by admitting to a crime they had not committed, just as the "Obedience to Authority" scenario placed people under immense pressure to harm another human being. Overcome by stress, fatigue, and trauma, young people were particularly vulnerable.[17] Delving into Kassin's work, I found he had much to say about stories. Criminal investigators, for example, do not stop at eliciting a confession. A full admission is required: that is, a story from the suspect that explains what they did, how, when, where, and why. As Kassin wrote, "A police-induced confession is like a Hollywood drama: scripted by the interrogator's theory of the case, shaped through questioning and rehearsal, directed by the questioner, and enacted by the suspect."[18]

One of my fellow jurors takes copious notes. Voicing her argument, she flips back and forth through the pages of a reporter's pad. Is she a journalist? Or perhaps a police officer? We soon gel as a group. Discussion is intense, and questions quickly pile up. Are there any holes in the two parties' respective stories? What exactly does "beyond reasonable doubt" mean? The provided legal glossary is consulted. We discover the expression refers to the standards that the prosecution's evidence must meet. It is connected to the fact that the defendant must be assumed innocent until proven guilty—often described as the golden thread that runs through the common-law system. I could not help thinking about Milgram's participants. I also could not help thinking about Kitty Genovese's neighbors. Should they not have been entitled to a presumption of innocence?

As our jury begins its deliberations, I review the video statements on my iPad. Who appears the most credible? The surgeon? Or his accuser? As I study facial expressions and gestures, I remind myself I am watching actors. As a filmmaker, I am more likely than most people to be drawn to audiovisual material. But I am not alone. Directors of live performance say that whenever there is a screen onstage, audiences will zoom in on it to the exclusion of all else. Our bias toward photographic evidence is powerful. Too often, we believe what we see. Yet films are never simply a record of captured scenes. Photographer and critic Alan Sekula observed that, by itself, an image merely presents the possibility of meaning. It is only by embedding photographic images in a given context that we can derive meaning.[19] Similarly, a jigsaw piece contributes to a scene only when placed in the puzzle; until then, it simply provides a clue, a glimpse of blue, a potential piece of sky. Visual evidence is only as good as the stories that accompany it. When introduced in courtroom settings, films are accompanied by narratives that too easily become conflated with the indexical nature of the images themselves.[20] Someone, somewhere is always constructing a story.

In late 1969, an exchange occurred between the CTV Television Network in Toronto and Stanley Milgram.[21] CTV was disappointed to learn that the *Obedience* documentary could not be cleared for television broadcast. In light of public debate regarding the massacre of civilians at My Lai during the Vietnam War, Milgram's documentary was particularly topical. Could he reconsider? Instead, Milgram proposed an alternative. One possibility was "to simulate the experiment by use of actors performing the typical experience of subjects in the experiment."[22] He would be glad to provide the apparatus and supervise. However, CTV declined. Instead, the broadcaster requested that the psychologist rerun the experiment with a small group of ordinary people. Otherwise, they would be accused of inventing reactions. The use of actors would be "less than real."[23] The phrase jumped out at me: "less than real."

The work of Swiss director and dramatist Milo Rau probes the limits of audiovisual evidence. His work is often the result of a lengthy process in which artistic creation is intertwined with historical or sociological research. In 2009, Rau invited a group of Romanian actors to reconstruct the violent revolution that occurred in their country. The resulting performance, *Die letzten Tage der Ceausescus (The Last Days of the Ceausescus)*, later made into a documentary, was based on a television broadcast of the trial of Nicolae and Elena Ceauşescu. Rau and his collaborators set out to re-enact the recording of the trial, frame by frame, but they soon discovered the limits of their historical source images. The camera angle showed only part of the courtroom. Inevitably, the audiovisual footage was not the whole picture—other accounts were needed.[24] Unlike many of his contemporaries, Rau does not dismiss realism; instead, he calls himself a "new realist." I am with him on this point. New realism engages with the real and, along the way, complicates what the term might mean—for example, by highlighting the gaps in stories rather than glossing over them.

I kept musing on the Canadian broadcaster's comments regarding the use of fictional elements as being "less than real." Why less?

Legal scholars have shown that the law is shaped through stories more than rules or policies. In real-life trials, the evidence presented can be unwieldy. A great deal of information is presented over a lengthy period, often in formats that make it difficult for jurors to connect details. The widely accepted "story model" of trials, devised by Pennington and Hastie, proposes that jurors make sense of evidence and arrive at their verdict by constructing a coherent story.[25] Stories are shaped so they can be understood by jurors and the wider public: "Stories organise the complex fragments of experience to reveal temporal linearity, elicit an epiphany ('Ah, now I see it how it was') and deliver 'motives,' 'harms,' 'guilt' and 'innocence.'"[26] Once that narrative is established, judges, jury, advocates, and expert witnesses can provide conflicting stories or introduce unspoken narratives that may override the official record.

Audience members often told the creators of *The Justice Syndicate* that the production "felt real." They wondered: How did it compare to an actual jury experience?[27] Louise Ellison and Vanessa Munro, sociologists who have worked with mock trials, observed that their participants were well aware they were involved in a role-play, and their decisions did not have "real" consequences. In their experience, role-play may well affect jurors' behavior, decisions, and verdicts in mock trials. Consequently, caution should be exercised in transposing the results of simulations to actual courtrooms. However, neither should the results of role-play be dismissed. Well-designed simulations still produce valuable insights.[28]

The two sociologists concluded that the legal instructions that mock jurors were given played a relatively minor role in constructing stories. More significant factors included the factual evidence available, observations regarding the credibility of the respective parties, and the individual juror's prior life experiences. In discussion with their peers, jurors were quick to identify gaps in the trial narratives, "as though seeking missing fragments of a picture they were attempting to piece together."[29] Ultimately, jurors filled in gaps in the story to make it more coherent and to justify a given verdict. Individual jurors may devise more than one coherent—that is, consistent, plausible, and complete—story. The jury's collective deliberations then become "a forum in which competing stories are articulated, defended, negotiated and reconfigured into an emergent master narrative" accepted by all, or at least the majority, of jurors.[30]

In room number—was it 202?—at Battersea Arts Centre, the hearing of our case reaches its conclusion. The nominated participants read the closing arguments for the prosecution and the defense. We vote one last time. Our verdict appears on screen: not guilty. For many of us, the burden of proof was simply insufficient. We were each given a mock broadsheet with a news article reporting our jury's verdict. An accompanying article outlined research on cognitive dissonance. In their debriefing session, Barnard and De Meyer outlined some of the psychology regarding decision-making that underpinned the production. They explained, "We wanted to immerse you in a playful environment of disagreement . . . [to] help you afterwards in the larger, real world of disagreement."[31] We often pay more attention to evidence that confirms our existing beliefs. This phenomenon has become even more marked in our era of social and political polarization, ramped up by social media platforms that can amplify divisions between groups of people.

To date, *The Justice Syndicate* has been run more than eighty times. Approximately 60 percent of the participant juries have found the defendant not guilty. According to the researchers, jurors who used soft-sell strategies such as open-ended questioning were far more effective in persuading other group members to their point of view than jurors who expressed their own opinions forcefully. Moreover, roughly half the participants did not change their vote from the first one taken ten minutes into the event. A further 37 percent changed their vote only once—usually to bring it in line with the emerging group consensus.[32] I belonged in the latter group. I was convinced that the surgeon was guilty from early on. Perhaps this had as much to do with my life experience as it did with the evidence presented? There were considerable disparities in power and status between a senior male medical professional and a young woman. I had little difficulty believing that the surgeon may have exploited this. The turning point in my verdict occurred when I realized not all my fellow jurors were convinced that the surgeon's guilt was established "beyond reasonable doubt." When I changed my vote, I felt a sense of relief.

One more aspect of our mock jury duty stayed with me. After observing many performances, the creative team for *The Justice Syndicate* felt a sense of optimism about juries. Most people wanted to arrive at the right decision rather than win the argument. Typically, they valued the contribution of those who disagreed with them since it enabled them to see the events from new perspectives and make more informed decisions: "People are kind and respectful to each other, including those they disagree with in a way that seems entirely different from the online space of social media . . . or combative mainstream political discourse."[33] The performances restored rather than diminished their faith in humanity—mine too.

More than a decade into my examination of social psychology's landmark "dramas as experiments," I find myself back at the beginning—pondering the nature of visual evidence and stories. This line of inquiry began with Milgram's iconic experiment and his film *Obedience* as a means of exploring how what we see (or do not see) shapes our understanding. Milgram, I discovered, played a critical role in inspiring the experiments of social psychology's golden era—those I think of as the Big Three: "Obedience to Authority," the "Bystander Effect," and the "Stanford Prison Experiment." Critically, Milgram's fingerprints were all over everything.

First, Milgram took Solomon Asch's "Conformity and Independence" experiments and ran with them. He observed that the experiments were living drama. The subject "was the hero but he does not know it."[34] Milgram added scale and topicality and increased the dramatic stakes to create his own "Obedience to Authority" series. (Along the way, much to Asch's distress, the "independence" aspect of the story was edited out of the picture.) Second, Milgram took advantage of his newfound authority to write about the Kitty Genovese murder and the "bystander" phenomenon. We may well have had a more dramatic set of bystander experiments if he had stayed on the case. Third, Zimbardo's "Stanford Prison Experiment" was devised in the shadow of Milgram's "Obedience to Authority" studies.

When I began this project, I was attracted strongly to the idea that psychology experiments could be both art and science. Over time, serious doubts arose. Too often, the art side of the equation was accorded a lesser value. Images, performance, and stories were treated simply as a means of communicating the discoveries and insights of science—or social science. However, art is not the servant of science; rather, it has its own history, ethics, and logic. As I have demonstrated, film and drama have their own research processes and methods. Photography and film are never simply visible facts. Stories and, more broadly, art have a high tolerance for ambiguity and contradiction. They are open to varying interpretations. Indeed, it is the very openness of stories that is central to their ability to act on the world. Art can spark conversations. It can enable us to see the world afresh. At its best, it brings people together. Art provides the companion stories that help us to navigate life and its complexities—as individuals, communities, and societies.

In 1963, literary agent Joan Davis rejected Milgram's short story "Article of Faith." The story, she reported, did not have enough of a narrative to succeed in a competitive market. She did not pull any punches. Phrases such as "her soft skin pulled him to the plan" were not only meaningless but also likely to annoy readers.[35] Davis kept sending out Milgram's work, but "Obedience to Authority" was the only story that sparked widespread interest. When would the manuscript be ready?

At the end of his experiments, Milgram was both excited and disturbed by his findings. I imagine him looking through his office window at night, musing on shadowy figures in the windows of neighboring apartments. Had he restricted his investigation to what could be measured? Did his results really concern cooperation rather than obedience? Was his experiment science or merely good theater? Milgram favored the latter. "In genuine science a mathematical or verbal description of the phenomenon is good enough," he wrote, "but the truth or significance of music, or a theatrical performance, or a painting, depends on direct confrontation and experiencing of the event."[36]

He scrawled his misgivings on yellow legal pads—typed them up and retyped them with carbon copies. He did not want us to overlook them. As I read those jottings about Milgram's doubts, my own investigation shifted gears. During the time I was working in the Stanley Milgram Papers archive, I walked all over the Yale University campus, shadowing the experimenter. One night, I found myself standing outside the Institute of Social Relations on Cedar Street, gazing up at his old office. Nothing seemed to have changed much. Keeping one eye out for the security guard, I slipped inside and took the rear stairs. Laboratories were clearly off limits. They were festooned with signs that read "Danger." or "Warning." However, around the academics' offices, things were a bit more relaxed. I was soon standing in Milgram's former office, gazing at silhouettes of people in nearby buildings. I tried to think my way into his head. If this were a scene in a film, it would be a series of shots and reverse shots. Detective. Evidence. Detective. Evidence. However, real-life investigations are rarely so well signposted.

I read my way through most of Patrick Modiano's books while I worked on this project. Why was I so drawn to Modiano's atmospheric narratives? His private detective narrators were all preoccupied by lost qualities of light, people, and places. They walked the streets of postwar Paris asking questions, taking notes, and making appointments. No detail was so small as to be unworthy of attention. I, too, was searching. I was searching for lost stories—specifically, social psychology's missing stories about people's capacity to cooperate, to come together in crises. Perhaps we should stop associating the word *story* with falsehood? Consider it instead as a means of building possible worlds?

Immersed in his *Obedience* drama, Milgram devised endless variations. He was like the showrunner on a hit series who does not know when to quit. Eventually, the National Science Foundation stepped in. It was a wrap. I had always wanted to track down participant 20XX, who pulled Milgram's shock generator from the wall socket to stop anyone from being hurt. It was time for me to pull the plug. At a certain point in shadowing a person of interest, you must let them go, wait as they disappear into the distance.

It is not quite that simple, of course. "A motel on the edge of town," I find scrawled in one of my notebooks that is more than a decade old. Once I struggled to decipher Milgram's handwritten notes. Now, it is my own handwriting I strain to decode. The notebooks contain musings and jottings for possible films. This one is all about Leon Festinger's *False Prophecy*.

"We live in a sea of stories," wrote Salman Rushdie. (Perhaps we can make that a sea of stories and images?) In the 1920s, Japanese novelist and essayist Jun'ichiro Tanazaki, had a similar vision. He imagined that all the world's stories survived on spools of film floating through the universe.[37] Wherever they were, according to Rushdie, stories "retained the ability to change, to become new versions of themselves, to join up with other stories and so become yet other stories."[38]

Film and screen media provide communities with one significant set of shared narrative resources. They are not fixed but always changing. Arguably, screen stories can adapt and change more quickly than the established narratives told in formal contexts such as legal proceedings. Stories, said Arthur Frank, have the capacity to narrate events in ways that leave open the interpretation of exactly what happened and how we should respond.[39] They are open to multiple understandings. We choose how to make use of the stories we encounter. We choose to live with them, tell them to others. We choose to forget stories, to rewrite them.

One of Modiano's narrators describes his unease at watching a comedy produced during the German occupation of France. His discomfort "stemmed from the film's particular luminosity, from the grain of the actual stock . . . the lighting was at once too bright and too dim, either stifling the voices or making the timbre louder, more disturbing."[40] He realized the film had been physically altered by the combined gaze of audiences. The grain of the film, the light, the voices of the actors had all shifted. It could never again be viewed as a light comedy. The same is true of Milgram's *Obedience* film and Zimbardo's photographic and video footage of the Stanford Prison Experiment. They can no longer be viewed as straightforward documentary evidence. They belonged to their time, not ours. Someone, somewhere is always telling a story.

Back at the Battersea Arts Centre, it is an astonishing experience to come together with eleven strangers (actually, make that ten, since my partner participated) for roughly the time it usually takes to see a movie—to engage in a discussion about one's deeply held beliefs around gender, power, justice, and responsibility and leave feeling so warmly toward each other.

It is time to let humanity off the hook—to widen our angle of vision and reauthor stories about the capacity of people to cooperate. Are we better than we think we are? I think this is what the evidence suggests. But you be the judge.

Acknowledgments

I am grateful to many people and institutions for their support, encouragement, and conversations over many years. Thanks to my colleagues Iqbal Barkat, Malcolm Choat, Maree Delofski, Bridget Griffen-Foley, Julie-Anne Long, Catherine Lumby, Peter McCarthy, Catriona McKenzie, Tom Murray, Karen Pearlman, Joseph Pugliese, Kate Rossmanith, Robert Sinnerbrink, Mark Wiggins, Rachel Yuen-Collingridge, and Jan Zwar at Macquarie University; Alex Munt at the University of Technology; Steven Maras at the University of Western Australia; David Carlin at RMIT University; Javer Lezaum at Oxford University; and J. J. Murphy at the University of Wisconsin–Madison. Particular thanks go to Adam Ganz at Royal Holloway, University of London, with whom I discussed much of this work along the way.

Special thanks to my social psychology collaborators. Alex Haslam at the University of Queensland, Steve Reicher at St. Andrews University, Stephen Gibson at Heriot Watt University, and Mark Levine at the University of Lancaster all shared their knowledge and insights regarding social psychology generously—I find their work inspiring.

I am deeply grateful to film historian and fellow filmmaker Charles Musser at Yale University, whose support enabled me to spend an extended period working with the Milgram Papers at the Sterling Library early in this project.

My thanks to Rachel Briscoe for conversations about the evolution of *The Justice Syndicate*. The project's key creative team comprised Rachel Briscoe and Dan Barnard (direction and dramaturgy) and Kris De Meyer, King's College, London, artistic associate (neuroscience).

Thanks to the Milgram estate and Michelle Marques for the privilege of working with the Milgram Archives and for permissions.

Thanks to Phillip Zimbardo for generously making available his archives to researchers and for permissions.

Thanks to the Faculty of Arts at Macquarie University for support that allowed me to visit archives and present at conferences.

I would like to acknowledge that this work has been supported by research grants from the Australian Research Council and the British Academy.

My thanks to many archivists for their support and assistance, particularly Cynthia Ostroff, Stephen Ross, and their colleagues in Manuscripts and Archives, Sterling Library, Yale University. My thanks to Josh Schneider, Special Collections, Stanford University; Neal Harmayer, Purdue University Archives and Special Collections; Lizette Royer Barton, Cummings Center for the History of Psychology, University of Akron; David McCartney and Denise Anderson, Special Collections and Archives, the University of Iowa Library; and the Manuscript Division, Library of Congress.

I am grateful to the organizers of the many conferences and public screenings at which some of this work has been discussed. These include the Milgram Symposium, Yale Law School; the Visible Evidence Conference; the British Psychology Society Social Psychology Section Conference; the Screenwriting Research Network Conference, Polin Museum of the History of Polish Jews, Warsaw; the European Association of Social Psychology General Meeting; the Powerhouse Museum, Sydney; the Australian Centre for Moving Image, and Antennae Documentary Film Festival.

My sincere thanks to Nicole Solano, executive editor, and her colleagues at Rutgers University Press for all their support and advice.

Last, special thanks to my partner and fellow writer, Noëlle Janaczewska, for her insights, comments, and suggestions on drafts throughout this project.

Notes

INTRODUCTION

1. Stefano Tani, *The Doomed Detective* (Carbondale: Southern Illinois University Press, 1984), 47.

2. Ivan Jablonka, *History Is a Contemporary Literature: Manifesto for the Social Sciences* (Ithaca, NY: Cornell University Press, 2018), xii.

3. Jablonka, 252.

4. Ron Mendall, *Probing into Cold Cases: A Guide for Investigators* (Springfield, IL: Charles C. Thomas, 2010), 235.

5. Timothy Garton Ash, "Truth Is Another Country," *The Guardian*, November 16, 2002, https://www.theguardian.com/books/2002/nov/16/fiction.society.

6. Jablonka, *History Is a Contemporary Literature*, 9.

7. Robert Darnton, *The Great Cat Massacre* (London: Hatchette, 2010), 12.

8. Theodor Adorno, "The Essay as Form," *New German Critique*, no. 32 (Spring–Summer, 1984), 160.

9. Arthur Frank, *The Wounded Storyteller* (Chicago: University of Chicago Press, 1995), 47.

10. See Thibault Le Texier, "Debunking the Stanford Prison Experiment," *American Psychologist* 74, no. 7 (2019): 823–839.

1. SETTING THE SCENE

1. Scott Curtis, Philippe Gauthier, Tom Gunning, and Joshua Yumibe, eds., *The Image in Early Cinema: Form and Material* (Bloomington: Indiana University Press, 2018), 9.

2. Brian Winston, *The Documentary Film Book* (London: Bloomsbury, 2019).

3. See Winston.

4. Charles Musser, "Documentary's Long Durée: Beginnings, Formations, Genealogies," *Nescus* 9, no. 2 (Autumn 2020): 21–50.

5. On shadow plays and picture storytellers, see Kathryn Millard, *Screenwriting in a Digital Era* (Basingstoke: Palgrave, 2014), 17–19.

6. Rick Altman, "From Lecturer's Prop to Industrial Product: The Early History of Travel Films," in *The Documentary Film Reader: History, Theory, Criticism*, ed. Jonathan Kahana (New York: Oxford University Press, 2016), 16.

7. Jonathan Marshall, *Performing Neurology: The Dramaturgy of Dr. Jean Martin Charcot* (New York: Palgrave Macmillan, 2016), 70.

8. Josef Brozek, ed., *Explorations in the History of Psychology* (East Brunswick, NJ: Associated University Presses, 1984), 198.

9. Arlie Belliveau, "Psychology's First Forays into Film," *Monitor on Psychology* 43, no. 5 (May 2012): 24, https://www.apa.org/monitor/2012/05/film.

10. Richard Lindstrom, "'They All Believe They Are Undiscovered Mary Pickfords': Workers, Photography and Scientific Management," *Technology and Culture* 41, no. 4 (October 2000): 725–751.

11. See Marsha Orgeron, "Multi-purposing Early Cinema: A Psychological Experiment Involving Van Bibber's Experiment," in *Beyond the Screen: Institutions, Networks and Publics of Early Cinema*, ed. Marta Braun, Charles Keil, Rob King, Paul S. Moore, and Louis Pelletier (New Barnet, UK: John Libbey, 2012), 154–159.

12. Edwin Boring, "Capacity to Report on Moving Pictures as Conditioned by Sex and Age: A Contribution to the Psychology of Testimony," *Journal of the American Institute of Criminal Law and Criminology* 6, no. 6 (March 1916): 820–834, https://www.jstor.org/stable/pdf/1133108.pdf.

13. Yuri Tsivian, *Early Cinema in Russia and Its Cultural Reception*, ed. Richard Taylor, trans. Alan Bodger (London: Routledge, 2014), 9.

14. Boring, "Capacity to Report on Moving Pictures," 822.

15. Emerson Manning, *Practical Instruction for Detectives* (Chicago: Frederick J. Drake and Co., 1921; Project Gutenberg, 2014).

16. Allan Langdale, *Hugo Münsterberg on Film: The Photoplay: A Psychological Study and Other Writings* (New York: Routledge, 2002), 204.

17. "Big Vital Thoughts Visualized on Screen," *Salt Lake City Herald*, April 23, 1919, 46.

18. Merle J. Moskowitz, "Hugo Münsterberg: A Study in the History of Applied Psychology," *American Psychologist* 32, no. 10 (October 1977): 824–842.

19. "Chronoscope Reads the Mind," *Argos (IN) Reflector*, November 7, 1907, 2.

20. "Chronoscope Reads the Mind," 2.

21. Charles Moore, "Yellow Psychology," *Law Notes* 11 (October 1907): 125.

22. See Jeremy Blatter, "Screening the Psychological Laboratory: Hugo Münsterberg, Psychotechnics, and the Cinema, 1892–1916," *Science in Context* 28, no. 1 (March 2015): 69–70.

23. See "To Ask Freud to Come Here," *New York Times*, December 21, 1924, 135; "Freud Rebuffs Goldwyn: Viennese Psychoanalyst Is Not Interested in Motion Picture Offer," *New York Times*, January 24, 1925, 13.

24. "Who's News Today," *Record* (Hackensack, NJ), March 21, 1938, 22.

25. See Sanford Gifford, "Freud at the Movies 1907–1925," in *Celluloid Couches, Cinematic Clients: Psychoanalysis and Psychotherapy in the Movies*, ed. Jerrold B. Brandell (New York: State University of New York Press, 2004), 150–153.

26. Herbert Gehr, "Arnold Gesell Studying Baby at Yale's Child Psychology Lab," 1947, Life Pictures Collection, http://images.google.com/hosted/life/od4349029c0282dc.html.

27. Scott Curtis, "'Tangible as Tissue': Arnold Gesell, Infant Behavior, and Film Analysis," *Science in Context* 24, no. 3 (October 2011): 417–442.

28. "Lewin and Observers Watching a Group of Children in the 'Project Room' Iowa," 1939, Frederick W. Kent Collection, University of Iowa Libraries, Iowa City, Iowa.

29. See Helmut Luck, "Kurt Lewin—Filmmaker," in *A Pictorial History of Photography*, ed. Charles Early, Helmut E. Luck, Rudolf Miller, and Wolfgang G. Bringmann (Chicago: Quintessence Publishing, 1997); Mel Elteren, "Kurt Lewin as Filmmaker and Methodologist," *Canadian Psychologist* 33, no. 3 (July 1992): 599–608.

30. Brozek, *Explorations in the History of Psychology*, 198.

31. Javier Lezaun, Fabian Muniesa, and Signe Vikkelsø, "Provocative Containment and the Drift of Social-Scientific Realism," *Journal of Cultural Economy* 6, no. 3 (2013): 281.

32. Javier Lezaun and Nerea Calvillo, "In the Political Laboratory: Kurt Lewin's Atmospheres," *Journal of Cultural Economy* 7, no. 4 (2014): 434–457.

33. Lezaun, Muniesa, and Vikkelsø, "Provocative Containment," 281.

34. "Kurt Lewin's Leadership Study," excerpt (1940s), Cummins Centre for the History of Psychology, https://www.youtube.com/watch?v=J7FYGn2NS8M.

35. See Ellen Herman, *The Romance of American Psychology: Political Culture in the Age of Experts* (Berkeley: University of California Press, 1995).

36. Noah Tsika, *Traumatic Imprints: Cinema, Military Psychiatry and the Aftermath of War* (Berkeley: University of California Press, 2018), 49.

37. *Introduction to Combat Fatigue*, U.S. Navy Training Film, 1944, https://www.youtube.com/watch?v=UN4Uj_4JKWA.

38. Tsika, *Traumatic Imprints*, 129.

39. James Maas and Kathleen Toivanen, "*Candid Camera* and the Behavioral Sciences," *AV Communications Review* 17, no. 3 (1969): 307.

40. Allen Funt, *Candidly: A Million Smiles Later* (New York: Barricade, 1994).

41. Funt, 23.

42. Funt, 24–26.

43. Funt, 30.

44. Funt, 43.

45. Stanley Milgram, *The Individual in a Social World: Essays and Experiments*, ed. Thomas Blass (London: Pinter and Martin, 2010), 393.

46. "Early *Candid Camera*," 1949, archive.org, https://archive.org/details/EarlyCandid Camera.

47. "Candid Camera," 1997, https://interviews.televisionacademy.com/shows/candid -camera.

48. Fred Nadis, "Citizen Funt: Surveillance as Cold War Entertainment," *Film and History: An Interdisciplinary Journal of Film and Television Studies* 37, no. 2 (2007): 14.

49. *Sherlock Jr.*, directed by Buster Keaton (1924; Los Angeles: Buster Keaton Productions and Fastforward Music, 2007), DVD.

50. See Leon Festinger, Henry Riecken, and Stanley Schachter, *When Prophecy Fails* (Mansfield, CT: Martino, 2011), for a full account of the field test and its methodology.

51. Anne Bogart, *What's the Story: Essays about Art, Theater and Storytelling* (Oxon: Routledge, 2014), 2.

52. Richard Evans and Jane Hildreth, "Psychologists View a *Candid Camera* Seminar," *American Psychologist* 19, no. 3 (1964): 210–211.

53. Evans and Hildreth, 211.

54. Harrison Engle, "Hidden Cameras and Human Behaviour: An Interview with Allen Funt," *Film Comment* 3, no. 4 (Fall 1965): 42.

55. Engle, 42.

56. Quoted in Thomas Blass, *The Man Who Shocked the World* (Cambridge, MA: Basic Books, 2004), 263–264.

2. "YOU'RE AN ACTOR NOW"

This chapter includes material from my 2014 article on Milgram's documentary published in the *Journal of Social Issues*. It builds on that article to consider screen performance, character, and narrative. See Kathryn Millard, "Revisioning Obedience: Exploring the Role of Milgram's Skills as a Filmmaker in Bringing His Shocking Narrative to Life," *Journal of Social Issues* 70, no. 3 (2014): 439–455.

1. Arlette Farge, *The Allure of the Archives* (New Haven, CT: Yale University Press, 2013), 8.

2. See Jerome Bruner, "The Narrative Construction of Reality," *Critical Inquiry* 18, no. 1 (Autumn 1991): 1–22; Jerome Bruner, *Making Stories: Law, Literature, Life* (Cambridge, MA: Harvard University Press, 2003).

3. Natalie Zemon Davis, *A Life of Learning: Hasker Lecture for 1997*, (American Council of Learned Societies, Occasional Paper No. 39, 8, https://www.acls.org/uploadedFiles/Publications/OP/Haskins/1997_NatalieZemonDavis.pdf.

4. Lynn Hunt, *History: Why It Matters* (Cambridge: Polity Press, 2018), 37.

5. Carlo Ginzburg, "On the Dark Side of History," *Eurozine*, July 11, 2013, https://www.eurozine.com/on-the-dark-side-of-history/.

6. See Umberto Eco, *Open Works* (Cambridge, MA: Harvard University Press, 1989).

7. Carlo Ginzburg, *Threads and Traces: True, False, Fictive* (Berkeley: University of California Press, 2012), 204.

8. Thomas Blass, *The Man Who Shocked the World: The Life and Legacy of Stanley Milgram* (New York: Basic Books, 2004), 78.

9. Stanley Milgram Papers (SMP), Sterling Library, Yale University, box 45, folder 160.

10. Nestar Russell, "Milgram's Obedience to Authority Experiments: Origins and Early Evolution," *British Journal of Social Psychology* 50 (2012): 140–162.

11. Stanley Milgram, *Obedience to Authority* (New York: Harper and Row, 1975), 15.

12. Paul Swann, *The British Documentary Film Movement 1926–46* (Cambridge: Cambridge University Press, 1989), 86.

13. SMP, box 43, folder 129.

14. SMP, box 46, folder 163.

15. Milgram, *Obedience to Authority*, 3.

16. SMP, box 45, folder 161.

17. Stanley Milgram, *The Individual in a Social World: Experiments and Essays*, ed. Thomas Blass (London: Pinter and Martin, 2010), 167.

18. SMP, box 46, folder 169.

19. Alan Elms, "Obedience in Retrospect," *Journal of Social Issues* 51, no. 3 (1995): 21–31.

20. Gina Perry's *Behind the Shock Machine: The Untold Story of the Notorious Milgram Psychology Experiments* (Melbourne: Scribe, 2012) places Fred Prozi in the version 5 run in October 1961, as Milgram claimed. My research places him in the film version run in late May 1962. See Millard, "Revisioning Obedience," 439–455.

21. Milgram, *The Individual in a Social World*, 392.

22. SMP, box 73, folder 381.

23. See, in particular, media scholar Anna McCarthy's insightful article "Stanley Milgram, Allen Funt and Me," in *Reality TV: Remaking Television Culture*, 2nd ed., ed. Susan Murray and Laurie Ouellette (New York: New York University Press, 2008), 23–43.

24. SMP, box 75, folder 436.

25. McCarthy, "Stanley Milgram, Allen Funt and Me," 37.

26. SMP, box 46, folder 440.

27. Warwick Mannon, *Call Northside 777: Book of the Film* (London: Hollywood Publications, 1948), 31.

28. Stanley Milgram, "Some Conditions of Obedience and Disobedience to Authority," *Human Relations* 18, no. 1 (1965): 67.

29. Milgram, 67.

30. Bill Nichols. *Introduction to Documentary* (Bloomington: Indiana University Press, 2010), 45.

31. Ilisa Barbash and Lucien Taylor, *Cross-Cultural Filmmaking: A Handbook for Making Documentary and Ethnographic Films and Videos* (Berkeley: University of California Press, 1997).

32. Nichols, *Introduction to Documentary*, 46.

33. Constantin Stanislavski, *Building a Character* (London: Bloomsbury, 2013).

34. Bruce McConchie, "Method Acting and the Cold War," *Theatre Survey* 41, no. 1 (2000): 47–67.

35. SMP, box 43, folder 129.

36. E. M. Forster, *Aspects of the Novel* (New York: Harcourt, 1955), 65–82.

37. Carl Plantinga, "Characterization and Character Engagement," in *Cognitive Theory and Documentary Film*, ed. Caitlin Brylla and Mette Kramer (London: Palgrave Macmillan, 2018), 122–124.

38. James Wood, *How Fiction Works* (New York: Random House, 2010), 83.

39. Wood, 83.

40. Milgram, *Obedience to Authority*, 73.

41. Milgram, 76.

42. Scott Eyman, *Hank and Jim: The Fifty-Year Friendship of Henry Fonda and James Stewart* (New York: Simon and Schuster, 2017), 172.

43. Plantinga, "Characterization and Character Engagement," 115–116.

44. Maureen Howard, "You Are There," in *Beyond Document: Essays in Nonfiction Film*, ed. Charles Warren (Middletown: Wesleyan University Press, 1996), 191–204.

45. SMP, box 122, folder 170.

3. NEW HAVEN NOIR

1. Stanley Milgram Papers (SMP), Sterling Library, Yale University, box 155, folder 3.

2. SMP, box 44.

3. SMP, box 155.

4. Peter Kramer, "Why Doctors Need Stories," *New York Times*, October 18, 2014, http://opinionator.blogs.nytimes.com/2014/10/18/why-doctors-need-stories/.

5. Jerome Bruner, *Making Stories: Law, Literature, Life* (Cambridge, MA: Harvard University Press, 2003).

6. Arthur Frank, *The Wounded Storyteller: Body, Illness, and Ethics* (Chicago: University of Chicago Press, 1995), 75.

7. *Judgement at Nuremberg*, directed by Stanley Kramer (1961; Los Angeles: United Artists, BFI, 2020), DVD.

8. *Perry Mason*, created by Erle Stanley Gardner (CBS, 1957–1966), television series.

9. *M*, directed by Fritz Lang (1931;Nero-Film AG, Berlin: BFI, 2014), DVD.

10. Patrick Modiano, *Missing Person* (London: Penguin Classics, 2019).

11. See Thomas Blass, *The Man Who Shocked the World: The Life and Legacy of Stanley Milgram* (New York: Basic Books, 2004), 127.

12. Ben Harris, "Key Words: A History of Debriefing in Social Psychology," in *The Rise of Experimentation in American Psychology*, ed. Jill G. Morawski (New Haven, CT: Yale University Press, 1988), 188–212.

13. SMP, box 155, folder 1.

14. SMP, box 155, folder 2.

15. Stanley Milgram, *Obedience to Authority* (New York: Harper and Row, 1975).

16. S, box 121, folder 127.

17. Nino Frank, "A New Kind of Police Drama," in *Film Noir Reader 2*, ed. Alain Silver and James Ursini (New York: Limelight, 1999), 15.

18. Frank, 16.

19. Paul Schrader, "Notes on Noir," *Film Comment* 8, no. 1 (Spring 1971): 8–13.

20. Ralph Blum, https://www.videomaker.com/article/c13/13548-create-detective-style-films-with-film-noir-lighting.

21. Sheri Biesen, *Blackout: World War II and the Origins of Film Noir* (Baltimore: Johns Hopkins University Press, 2005).

22. See Winfried Fluck, "Crime, Guilt, and Subjectivity in Film Noir," *Amerikastudien/American Studies* 46, no. 3 (2001): 379–408.

23. Ivan Jablonka, *History Is a Contemporary Literature: Manifesto for the Social Sciences* (Ithaca, NY: Cornell University Press, 2018).

24. SMP, box 119, folder 1.

25. SMP box 155, folder 3.

26. Lang, *M*.

27. SMP, box 155, folder 6.

28. SMP, box 120, folder 20 (0919).

29. SMP, box 155, folder 3.

30. SMP, box 155, folder 3.

31. Ron Mendall, *Probing into Cold Cases: An Investigators' Manual* (Springfield, IL: Charles Thomas, 2010), 28.

32. SMP, box 155, folder 3.

33. Biesen, *Blackout*.

34. See Jean-Louis Comolli, "Fatal Rendezvous," in *Cinema and the Shoah*, ed. Jean-Michel Frodon, trans. Anna Harrison and Tom Mes (Albany: State University of New York Press, 2010), 53–54; John Michalczyk, *Filming the End of the Holocaust: Allied Documentaries, Nuremberg and the Liberation of the Concentration Camps* (London: Bloomsbury, 2014).

35. Stanley Milgram, "An Experimenter's Dilemma," unpublished note (n.d.), SMP, box 62, folder 126.

36. SMP, Milgram, "An Experimenter's Dilemma."

37. Frank, *Wounded Storyteller*, 75.

4. GOOD OR BAD SAMARITANS?

1. John Kotre, "Experiments as Parables," *American Psychologist* 47, no. 5 (May 1992): 672–673.

2. "Lonely Street Based on Real Murder," *Calgary (AB) Herald*, July 18, 1964, 28.

3. See Alain Silver and James Silver, "Docu-noir," in *Film Noir*, ed. Paul Duncan and Jürgen Müller (Cologne: Taschen, 2017), 99–114; Jason Mittel, *Genre and Television: From Cop Shows to Cartoons in American Culture Television Genres* (New York: Routledge, 2004), 94–152.

4. "Queens Woman Is Stabbed to Death in Front of Home," *New York Times*, March 14, 1964, 26.

5. See Jim Rasenberger, "Kitty, 40 Years Later," *New York Times*, February 8, 2004; Rachel Manning, Mark Levine, and Alan Collins, "The Kitty Genovese Murder and the Social Psychology of Helping: The Parable of the 38 Witnesses," *American Psychologist* 62, no. 6 (2007): 555–562; Nicholas Lemann, "A Call for Help: What the Kitty Genovese Story Really Means," *New Yorker*, March 3, 2014, https://www.newyorker.com/magazine/2014/03/10/a-call-for-help.

6. "Queens Woman Is Stabbed to Death in Front of Home,'26.

7. Thomas Pugh and Richard Henry, "Knifed Barmaid Dies in Mystery," *New York Daily News*, March 14, 1964, 128.

8. Michael Keaton, "Witnesses Describe Stabber of Barmaid," *New York Daily News*, March 15, 1964, 265.

9. Robert Parrella, "Help Cry Ignored, Girl Dies of Knifing," *New York Herald Tribune*, March 14, 1964.

10. Abe Rosenthal, *Thirty-Eight Witnesses* (1968; repr., New York: Skyhouse, 2016), 56.

11. Martin Gansberg, "38 Watch Killer Stalk, Stab Prey," *New York Times*, March 27, 1964, 1.

12. Arthur J. Lurigio, "Crime Narratives, Dramatizations, and the Legacy of the Kitty Genovese Murder," *Criminal Justice and Behavior* 42, no. 7 (July 2015): 782–789.

13. Association of Crime Scene Reconstruction by-laws quoted in Ross Gardner and Tom Bevel, *Practical Crime Scene Analysis and Reconstruction* (Boca Raton, FL: CRC Press, 2009), 1.

14. *CSI: Crime Scene Investigation*, season 1, episode 10, directed by Thomas J. Wright, aired December 22, 2000, on CBS.

15. Luke May, *Scientific Murder Investigation* (Seattle: Institute of Scientific Criminology, 1933), 9.

16. Tom Bevel and Ross Gardner, *Bloodstain Pattern Analysis with an Introduction to Crime Scene Reconstruction* (Boca Raton, FL: CRC Press, 2008), 6.

17. Abe Rosenthal, "Apathy Is Puzzle in Queens Killing," *New York Times*, March 28, 1964.

18. "TV Called Factor in Slaying Apathy; Psychiatrist Gives Views on Witnesses in Queens," *New York Times*, April 12, 1964.

19. Rosenthal, *Thirty-Eight Witnesses*, 45.

20. See "The Apathetic American," *Boston Globe*, August 9, 1964, 51.

21. "38 Witnesses May Be a Film," *New York Times*, December 18, 1964.

22. *Perry Mason*, season 9, episode 11, directed by Jesse Hibbs, aired November 21, 1965, on CBS.

23. John Darley and Bibb Latane, "When Will People Help in a Crisis?," in *Readings in Social Psychology Today*, ed. James McConnell (Del Mar, CA: CRM Books, 1970), 3–7.

24. Thomas Buckley, "Rape Victim's Screams Draw 40, but No One Acts," *New York Times*, May 6, 1964.

25. "Girl Assaulted; Crowd Stands By," *Democrat and Chronicle* (Rochester, NY), May 6, 1964, 7.

26. "Court Told 40 Ignored Girl's Pleas," *Morning News* (Wilmington, DE), May 6, 1964, 25; "N.Y.: Where No One Cares," *Odessa (TX) American*, May, 1964, 27.

27. "10 Passengers See Youth Slain," *Los Angeles Times*, March 14, 1965, 29.

28. Emanuel Perlmutter, "Police Ride IND Seeking Witnesses," *New York Times*, March 15, 1965, 36.

29. "Boy's Subway Ride to Killing Nobody Saw," *New York Daily News*, March 14, 1965, 45.

30. "Study of a Slaying Brings Award to 2," *New York Times*, December 29, 1988, 31.

31. Irving Piliavin, Judith Rodin, and Jane Piliavin, "Good Samaritanism: An Underground Phenomenon?," *Journal of Personality and Social Psychology* 13, no. 4 (1969): 280–299.

32. Delos Smith, "Tests Drew Good Samaritans," *Cedar Rapids, Iowa Gazette*, May 17, 1970, 16.

33. Stanley Milgram and Paul Hollander, "The Murder They Heard," *Nation* 198, no. 25 (June 15, 1964): 602–604.

34. Carol Travis, "The Frozen World of the Familiar Stranger," *Psychology Today* 8 (June 1974): 71–73, 80, 86–88.

35. Loudon Wainwright, "The Dying Girl That No One Helped," *Life*, April 10, 1964, 21.

36. *The Fugitive*, created by Roy Huggins (QM Productions and United Artists Television, 1963–1967).

37. Frances Cherry, *The Stubborn Particulars of Social Psychology* (Florence, KY: Taylor and Francis/Routledge, 2014).

38. Rasenberger, "Kitty, 40 Years Later."

39. Quoted in Beryl Benderly, "Psychology's Tall Tales," *gradPsych* 9 (2012): 20, https://www.apa.org/gradpsych/2012/09/tall-tales

40. *Death Scream*, directed by Richard T. Heffron (Los Angeles: Robert Stigwood Organization, 1975), https://www.youtube.com/watch?v=kiqqRwXKpdM.

41. *The Witness*, directed by James Solomon (2015; New York: Film Rise, 2016), DVD.

42. Bill Nichols, *Introduction to Documentary* (Bloomington: Indiana University Press, 2017), 33.

43. Rebecca Solnit, "To Break the Story, You Must Break the Status Quo," *Lithub*, May 12, 2016, https://lithub.com/to-break-the-story-you-must-break-the-status-quo/.

44. Stefani Tani, *The Doomed Detective* (Carbondale: Southern Illinois University Press, 1984), 35–41.

45. Richard Philpot, Lasse Suonperä Liebst, Mark Levine, Wim Bernasco, and Marie Rosenkrantz Lindegaard, "Would I Be Helped? Cross-National CCTV Footage Shows That Intervention Is the Norm in Public Conflicts," *American Psychologist* 71, no. 1 (2019), 66–75; and Charlotte Bloch, Lasse Suonperä Liebst, Poul Poder, Jasmin Maria Christiansen, and Maria Bruvik Heinskou, "Caring Collectives and Other Forms of Bystander Helping Behavior in Violent Situations," *Current Sociology* 66, no. 7 (2018): 1049–1069.

46. John Drury, Chris Cocking, and Steve Reicher, "The Nature of Collective Resilience: Survivor Reactions to the 2005 London Bombings," *International Journal of Mass Emergencies and Disasters* 27, no. 1 (2009): 66–95.

47. See Nicholas Christakis, *Blueprint: The Evolutionary Origins of a Good Society* (New York: Little Brown Spark, 2019); Jamil Zaki, *The War for Kindness: Building Empathy in a Fractured World* (New York: Crown, 2019).

5. DOING TIME

1. Philip G. Zimbardo, Advertisement for Stanford Prison Experiment, 1973, "Prison Study: Setting Up," 1999–2021, https://www.prisonexp.org/setting-up.

2. *Punishment Park*, directed by Peter Watkins (1971; New York: Project X and New Yorker Video, 2005), DVD.

3. Philip G. Zimbardo, "Stanford Prison Experiment," 1999–2021, https://www.prison exp.org/.

4. See "The Stanford Prison Experiment (2015)," Internet Movie Database, 2020, https://www.imdb.com/title/tt0420293/.

5. "Prison Test Halted—Too Brutal," *San Francisco Examiner*, August 20, 1971, 3; "Prison Experiment Proves Too Realistic," *Daily Herald* (Provo, UT), Sunday, August 22, 1971, 33.

6. "Prison Experiment Just Too Realistic," *Arizona Republic*, August 21, 1971, 3.

7. "Ex-Convict Teaches Prison Psychology," *Times Standard* (Eureka, CA), July 31, 1971, 5; "A Teacher from Another World," *San Francisco Examiner*, August 2, 1971, 3.

8. Leon Festinger quoted in Augustine Brannigan, *The Rise and Fall of Social Psychology: The Use and Misuse of the Experimental Method* (New York: Aldine DeGruyer, 2004) 37.

9. See "The BBC Prison Study," BBC, 2008, http://www.bbcprisonstudy.org.

10. Lisa Kerrigan, "Social Experiment TV," http://www.screenonline.org.uk/tv/id/1387837/index.html.

11. "The BBC Prison Study."

12. S. Alexander Haslam and Stephen D. Reicher, "When Prisoners Take Over the Prison: A Social Psychology of Resistance," *Personality and Social Psychology Review* 16, no. 2 (2018): 158.

13. "BBC Halts Prison Experiment," *The Guardian*, January 24, 2002, https://www.theguardian.com/uk/2002/jan/24/bbc.socialsciences.

14. "The BBC Prison Study."

15. "The BBC Prison Study."

16. "Shocking Experiment Recreated for TV," BBC News, May 14, 2002, http://news.bbc.co.uk/2/hi/entertainment/1986889.stm.

17. Julia Galef, "Thibault Le Texier on 'Debunking the Stanford Prison Experiment,'" *Rationally Speaking Podcast*, episode 241, October 14, 2019, http://rationallyspeaking podcast.org/show/rs-241-thibault-le-texier-on-debunking-the-stanford-prison-e.html.

18. Thibault Le Texier, *Histoire d'un menage* (Paris: La Decouverte, 2018).

19. Link to "Supplemental Material A: Comparison of the Rules of the Toyon Hall Experiment and of the SPE," in Thibault Le Texier, "Debunking the Stanford Prison Experiment," *American Psychologist* 74, no. 7 (2019): 823.

20. See Warden, quoted by Le Texier, "Debunking the Stanford Prison Experiment": 829.

21. Archival audio recording provided by Le Texier available at Brian Resnick, "The Stanford Prison Experiment Is Based on Lies. Hear Them for Yourself," *Vox*, June 14, 2018, https://www.vox.com/science-and-health/2018/6/14/17464516/stanford-prison-experiment-audio.

22. Benedict Carey, "Psychology Itself Is under Scrutiny," *New York Times*, July 16, 2018, https://www.nytimes.com/2018/07/16/health/psychology-studies-stanford-prison.html.

23. Rebecca Solnit, "To Break the Story, You Must Break the Status Quo," *LitHub*, May 26, 2018, https://lithub.com/to-break-the-story-you-must-break-the-status-quo/.

24. See Sharon Ghamari-Tabrizi, "Simulating the Unthinkable: Gaming Future War in the 1950s and 1960s," *Social Studies of Science* 30, no. 2 (April 2000): 173–179.

25. Philip Zimbardo, "The Effect of Effort and Improvisation on Self-Persuasion Produced by Role-Playing," *Journal of Experimental Social Psychology* 1, no. 2 (1965): 103–120.

26. Zimbardo, 103.

27. Krysia Yardley-Matwiejczuk, *Role-Play: Theory and Practice* (London: Sage, 1997), 1.

28. See Theodore Shank, *American Alternative Theatre* (New York: Grove Press, 1982).

29. *The Brig*, directed by Jonas Mekas (1964; New York: Re:voir, 2012), DVD.

30. Kenneth Brown, *The Brig: A Concept for Theatre or Film* (New York: Hill and Wang, 1965), 49–50.

31. Brown, 44.

32. Brown, 45–47.

33. Judith Malina, "Directing *The Brig*," in Brown, *The Brig*, 92–95.

34. Malina, 92–95.

35. Jonas Mekas, "Shooting *The Brig*," DVD notes, reprinted in *Village Voice*, October 1, 1964.

36. Mekas.

37. Julian Beck, "Storming the Barricades," in Brown, *The Brig*, 1–35.

38. "Prisoner Rules," Philip G. Zimbardo, 2020, http://pdf.prisonexp.org/rules.pdf.

39. *The War Game*, directed by Peter Watkins (1965; London: British Film Institute, 2016), DVD.

40. Peter Watkins, "The War Game," 2019, http://pwatkins.mnsi.net/warGame.htm.

41. Peter Watkins, "Punishment Park and Dissent in the West," *Literature and Film Quarterly* 4, no. 4 (Fall 1976): 292–302.

42. See *Punishment Park*, DVD notes, reprinted from Joseph A. Gomez, *Peter Watkins* (Boston: Twayne, 1979).

43. Anne Bogart, *A Director Prepares: Seven Essays on Art and Theatre* (New York: Routledge, 2001), 26.

44. See John Cook, "Don't Forget to Look into the Camera: Peter Watkins's Approach to Directing with Facts," *Studies in Documentary Film* 4, no. 3 (2010): 236; Peter Watkins, "The Media Crisis: A Perspective by Peter Watkins," Tate, September 2012, https://www.tate.org.uk/whats-on/tate-modern/peter-watkins-films-1964-99/media-crisis-perspective-peter-watkins.

6. CRIME SCENES

1. Philip Zimbardo, *The Lucifer Effect: How Good People Turn Evil* (London: Rider, 2007), 23.

2. Zimbardo, 23–39; Philip Zimbardo, "The Story," 2020, https://www.prisonexp.org/the-story.

3. John Yorke, *Into the Woods: How Stories Work and Why We Tell Them* (London: Penguin, 2014).

4. Zimbardo, *The Lucifer Effect*, 27–29.

5. Zimbardo, 23–25.

6. "Violence," *San Francisco Examiner*, June 15, 1969, 252–253.

7. "Crime: Diary of a Vandalized Car," *Time*, February 28, 1969.

8. "Crime."

9. Zimbardo, *The Lucifer Effect*; Philip Zimbardo, "The Human Choice: Individuation, Reason, and Order versus Deindividuation, Impulse, and Chaos," in Nebraska Symposium on Motivation, ed. W.J. Arnold and D. Devine (Lincoln: University of Nebraska Press, 1969), 17:237–307.

10. "Violence," 252–253.

11. Philip Zimbardo, "A Field Experiment in Auto-Shaping," in *Vandalism*, ed. Collin Ward (London: Architectural Press, 1973).

12. "Violence," 252–253.

13. "Stunned Students View 12-Storey Death Plunge," *Sapulpa (OK) Daily Herald*, September 27, 1967, 1.

14. See Robert Wallace, "Crime in the U.S.," and Gordon Parks "Atmosphere of Crime," *Life*, September 9, 1957, 47–70.

15. Wallace, "Crime in the U.S.," 47.

16. See Sarah Hermanson Meister, Nicole Fleetwood, and Bryan Stevenson, *Gordon Parks: The Atmosphere of Crime* (Göttingen: Steidl, Gordon Parks Foundation, 2020).

17. Bill Shapiro, "Six Pictures: Gordon Parks' 'Atmosphere of Crime,'" *Blind*, December 23, 2020, https://www.blind-magazine.com/en/stories/1161/Six-Pictures-Gordon-Parks -Atmosphere-Of-Crime.

18. Shapiro.

19. James Wilson and George Kelling, "Broken Windows: Neighborhoods and Public Safety," *Atlantic*, March 1982, 29–38.

20. Bernard Harcourt and Jens Ludwig, "Broken Windows: New Evidence from New York City and a Five-City Social Experiment," *University of Chicago Law Review* 73 (2006): 271–320.

21. Shankar Vedantam, Chris Benderev, Tara Boyle, Renee Klahr, Maggie Penman, and Jennifer Schmidt, "How a Theory of Crime and Policing Was Born, and Went Terribly Wrong," *Hidden Brain*, November 1, 2016, https://www.npr.org/2016/11/01 /500104506/broken-windows-policing-and-the-origins-of-stop-and-frisk-and-how -it-went-wrong.

22. See Bench Ansfield, "The Broken Windows of the Bronx: Putting the Theory in Its Place," *American Quarterly* 72, no. 1 (March 2020): 103–127.

23. George Kelling quoted in Vedantam et al., "How a Theory of Crime and Policing Was Born."

24. "Violence," 252–253.

25. "Violence," 252–253.

26. *The Birth of a Nation*, directed by D. W. Griffith (1915; New York: Kino Classics, 2011), DVD.

27. These photographs were exhibited and published after Arbus's suicide in 1971. Selected notebook entries can be read in Elizabeth Sussman and Doon Arbus, eds., *Diane Arbus: A Chronology 1927–1971* (New York: Aperture, 2011).

28. Philip Zimbardo (@PhilZimbardo), "A personal journey from evil to heroism," Twitter, August 31, 2018, 5:37 p.m., https://twitter.com/philzimbardo/status/103564264938 4955904?lang=en.

29. "The Hooded Man. Sergeant Ivan Frederick 2003," in *100 Photographs: The Most Influential Images of All Time* (New York: Time Home Entertainment, 2016), 158.

30. Zimbardo, *Lucifer Effect*, 19–20.

31. See illustration 63 in Errol Morris, *Believing Is Seeing (Observations on the Mysteries of Photography)* (New York: Penguin, 2014), 101.

32. Fred Ritchin, *After Photography* (New York: Norton, 2019), 86.

33. Zimbardo, *Lucifer Effect*, 344.

34. Zimbardo, 372.

35. Jamie Wilson, "Eight Years for Soldier Who Abused Prisoners," *The Guardian*, October 23, 2004, https://www.theguardian.com/world/2004/oct/22/usa.iraq.

36. Kristin Thomas and David Bordwell, "Errol Morris: Boy Detective," November 4, 2020, http://www.davidbordwell.net/blog/2010/11/04/errol-morris-boy-detective/.

37. Thomas and Bordwell.

38. Livia Bloom, ed., *Errol Morris: Interviews* (Jackson: University of Mississippi Press, 2010), 246.

39. See Kathryn Millard, *Screenwriting in a Digital Era* (Basingstoke, UK: Palgrave Macmillan, 2014), 63–76.

40. Morris, *Believing Is Seeing*, 118.

41. Bill Nichols, "Feelings of Revulsion and the Limits of Academic Discourse," *Jump Cut*, no. 52 (summer 2010), https://www.ejumpcut.org/archive/jc52.2010/sopNichols/text.html.

42. Linda Williams, "The Forcible Frame in Errol Morris's Standard Operating Procedure," *Camera Obscura* 25, no. 1 (73) (May 2010): 32.

43. Philip Zimbardo, Craig Haney, W. Curtis Banks, and David Jaffe, "The Stanford Prison Experiment: A Simulation of the Psychology of Imprisonment conducted August 1971 at Stanford University," slide/tape narration, n.d., https://web.stanford.edu/dept/spec_coll/uarch/exhibits/Narration.pdf.

44. John Berger, *Bento's Sketchbook* (London: Verso, 2015).

45. John Berger, Sven Blomberg, Chris Fox, Michael Dibb, and Richard Hollis, *Ways of Seeing* (London: BBC, 1972), 8.

7. RESTAGING THE PSYCHOLOGY EXPERIMENT

1. Stanley Milgram and Thomas Blass, eds., *The Individual in a Social World: Essays and Experiments*, 3rd ed. (London: Pinter and Martin, 2010), xxviii.

2. See Katie Mitchell, *The Director's Craft: A Handbook for the Theatre* (Oxon: Routledge, 2010), 44–51.

3. Mitchell, 47.

4. *The Milgram Re-enactment*, directed by Rod Dickinson (Glasgow: Centre for Contemporary Art, 2002). See video documentation at https://www.roddickinson.net/pages/milgram/performance.php.

5. Vivienne Gaskin, "Subjects in Search of an Author," in *The Milgram Re-enactment: Essays on Rod Dickinson's Re-enactment of Stanley Milgram's Obedience to Authority Experiment in Collaboration with Graeme Edler*, ed. Steve Rushton (Maastricht, Netherlands: Jan van Eyck Academie, 2003), 13.

6. Rod Dickinson, "The Milgram Re-enactment," Projects/Artworks, 2002. https://www.roddickinson.net/pages/milgram/project-synopsis.php.

7. Gaskin, "Subjects in Search of an Author," 9.

8. Ali MacGilp, "Interview with Rod Dickinson: The Milgram Re-enactment," *Art Vehicle*, 2002.

9. *Shock Room*, directed by Kathryn Millard (Sydney: Charlie Productions, 2015; Ronin Films, 2016), DVD.

10. Cesare Zavattini, "Some Ideas on the Cinema," *Sight and Sound* 23, no. 2 (1953): 64–69.

11. William Gamson, Bruce Fireman, and Steve Rytina, *Encounters with Unjust Authority* (Homewood, IL: Dorsey Press, 1982).

12. See *Random 8*, directed by Kathryn Millard (Sydney: Charlie Productions, 2012; Ronin Films, 2012), DVD.

13. See Murray Pomerance, *The Eyes Have It: Cinema and the Reality Effect* (New Brunswick, NJ: Rutgers University Press, 2013).

14. Hanna Schenkel, "Reclaiming Resistance: *Shock Room* and the Problem of Documentary Truth," *Metro* 188 (2015): 81.

15. Bill Nichols, "Documentary Reenactments: A Paradoxical Temporality That Is Not One," *DOK Revue*, April 28, 2014, https://www.dokrevue.cz/en/clanky/documentary-reenactments-a-paradoxical-temporality-that-is-not-one.

16. Schenkel, "Reclaiming Resistance," 81.

17. *Experimenter: The Stanley Milgram Story*, directed by Michael Almereyda (New York: Intrinsic Value Films Productions, 2015; Rialto, 2016), DVD. Official website: http://experimentermovie.com.

18. Eric Hynes, "Artist Spotlight, Cinematic Experiments: Michael Almereyda Is Back with Heady Psych Drama *Experimenter*," Sundance Institute, October 13, 2015, https://www.sundance.org/blogs/artist-spotlight/cinematic-experiments—michael-almereyda-is-back-with-heady-psych-drama-experimenter.

19. "Creating the Visual World of *Experimenter*," *Production Hub*, November 2, 2015.

20. Jonathon Law, *The Methuen Drama Dictionary of the Theatre* (London: Methuen, 2013), 120.

21. "'Experimenter' Star Peter Sarsgaard on Stanley Milgram's Radical Work," NPR, October 18, 2015, https://www.npr.org/2015/10/18/449662993/-experimenter-star-peter-sarsgaard-on-stanley-milgrim-s-radical-work.

22. See Stephen Gibson, *Arguing, Resisting and Defying: A Rhetorical Perspective on Stanley Milgram's Obedience Experiments* (Cambridge: Cambridge University Press, 2019).

23. *Experiment 20*, directed by Kathryn Millard (2018), https://www.theguardian.com/film/video/2018/mar/12/present-traces-experiment-20-video.

24. Stanley Milgram, *Obedience to Authority* (New York: Harper and Row, 1974), 84.

25. Milgram, 85.

26. Will Hammon and Dan Steward, eds., *Verbatim, Verbatim: Contemporary Documentary Theatre* (London: Oberon Books, 2010).

27. See Caroline Borge, "Basic Instinct: The Science of Evil," ABC News, April 27, 2007, https://abcnews.go.com/Primetime/story?id=2765416&page=1.

28. Adam Ledger, "'The Thrill of Doing It Live': Devising and Performing Katie Mitchell's International 'Live Cinema' Productions," in *Contemporary Approaches to Adaptation in Theatre*, ed. Kara Reilly (London: Palgrave Macmillan, 2017), 69–90.

8. "I WAS THE SYSTEM"

1. Patrick Modiano, *Pedigree* (London: MacLehose Press, 2015), 38.

2. J. Chamberlin, "Media Picks: Philip G. Zimbardo, PhD. Two Thumbs Up: Zimbardo's Favorite Flicks," *gradPSYCH Magazine*, September 2011, https://www.apa.org /gradpsych/2011/09/media-picks.

3. Tim Talbot, *The Stanford Prison Experiment Script*, March 25, 2006, in Philip G. Zimbardo Papers, Stanford University, https://purl.stanford.edu/kv784nx1963.

4. Talbot, cover.

5. Dan McAdams, *The Redemptive Self: Stories Americans Live By* (New York: Oxford University Press, 2013), 9–13.

6. See Robert McKee, *Story: Substance, Structure, Style, and the Principles of Screenwriting* (New York: HarperCollins, 1997).

7. Chamberlin, "Media Picks."

8. Chamberlin.

9. "Making *The Stanford Prison Experiment*: An Interview with Kyle Patrick Alvarez," *Lunacy*, November 28, 2017, https://lunacyproductions.com/making-stanford -prison-experiment-interview-kyle-patrick-alvarez/.

10. Jamie Chamberlin, "Social Psychology on the Silver Screen," *Monitor on Psychology* 46, no. 3 (March 2015), https://www.apa.org/monitor/2015/03/upfront-screen.html; Chris Petrikin and Michael Fleming, "Fox Looks to Pick Up DiCaprio 'Prison' Pic," *Variety*, February 4, 1999, https://variety.com/1999/film/news/fox-looks-to-lock-up-dicaprio -prison-pic-1117491013/.

11. Hugh Hart, "*Das Experiment* Comes with Its Own Set of Trials," *LA Times*, September 18, 2002, https://www.latimes.com/archives/la-xpm-2002-sep-18-et-hugh18 -story.html.

12. "*Das Experiment* Film and 1971 Stanford Prison Study Transcript," *Morning Edition*, NPR, September 18, 2002.

13. Peter Rollins, ed., *The Columbia Companion to American History on Film* (New York: Columbia University Press, 2013), 454.

14. Michael Fleming, "'Prison' Term for Maverick: McQuarrie to Helm 'Experiment,'" *Variety*, November 5, 2006, https://variety.com/2006/film/news/prison-term-for-maverick -1117953363/.

15. "Judge Orders Madonna Film Company to Settle Fight on Prisoner Abuse Movie," Fox News, February 27, 2007, https://www.foxnews.com/story/judge-orders-madonna -film-company-to-settle-fight-on-prisoner-abuse-movie.

16. Jeanne Veillette Bowerman, "Line between Good and Evil: Tim Talbot on Writing 'Stanford Prison Experiment,'" *Script Magazine*, July 15, 2015, https://scriptmag .com/features/tim-talbott-stanford-prison-experiment.

17. Talbot, *Stanford Prison Experiment Script*, cover.

18. Talbot, 5.

19. Arthur Frank, *Letting Stories Breathe: A Socio-Narratology* (Chicago: University of Chicago Press, 2010), 9.

20. See *Celluloid Ceiling* reports, Centre for Study of Women in Film and Television, https://womenintvfilm.sdsu.edu/research/.

21. Talbot, *Stanford Prison Experiment Script*.

22. "Making *The Stanford Prison Experiment*."

23. "Making *The Stanford Prison Experiment.*"

24. Erving Goffman, *The Presentation of Self in Everyday Life* (New York: Doubleday, 1959), 119–132.

25. Talbot, *Stanford Prison Experiment Script*, 19.

26. See Ben Blum, "The Lifespan of a Lie," *Medium*, June 7, 2018, https://gen.medium .com/the-lifespan-of-a-lie-d869212b1f62.

27. Philip Zimbardo, *The Lucifer Effect: How Good People Turn Evil* (London: Rider, 2007), 33.

28. Zimbardo, 209.

29. Hugh Hart, "How the Makers of 'The Stanford Prison Experiment' Recreated the Famously Disturbing Experiment," *fastcompany*, July 22, 2015, https://www.fastcompany .com/3048706/how-the-makers-of-the-stanford-prison-experiment-recreated-the -famously-disturbing-experimen.

30. McAdams, *Redemptive Self*, 210.

31. Siri Hustvedt, "Notes on Seeing," in *Living, Thinking, Looking: Essays*, ed. Siri Hustvedt (London: Picador, 2012), 231.

32. Talbot, *Stanford Prison Experiment Script.*

33. For a discussion of this version of the redemption story, see Shadd Maruna, *Making Good: How Ex-Convicts Reform and Rebuild Their Lives* (Washington, DC: American Psychological Association, 2001), 85–91.

34. U.S. Congress, Senate Committee on the Judiciary Subcommittee to Investigate Juvenile Delinquency, *The Detention and Jailing of Juveniles: Hearings Before the Subcommittee to Investigate Juvenile Delinquency of the Committee on the Judiciary, United States Senate, Ninety-Third Congress, First Session, Pursuant to S. Res. 56, Section 12 . . . September 10, 11, and 17, 1973* (Washington, DC: U.S. Government Printing Office, 1974).

35. Talbot, *Stanford Prison Experiment Script.*

36. Zimbardo, *Lucifer Effect*, 457.

37. Zimbardo, 457.

38. Sam Girgus, *Levinas and the Cinema of Redemption* (New York: Columbia University Press, 2010), 25.

39. Hart, "How the Makers."

40. Peter Brooks, *Troubling Confessions: Speaking Guilt in Law and Literature* (Chicago: University of Chicago Press, 2010), 9.

41. McAdams, *Redemptive Self*, 196.

42. Talbot, *Stanford Prison Experiment Script*, cover.

43. U.S. Congress, *Hearings Before Subcommittee No. 3 of the Committee on the Judiciary, House of Representatives, Ninety-second Congress, First [and Second] Session on Corrections Practices, Their Faults and Shortcomings* (Washington, DC: U.S. Government Printing Office, 1971).

9. SHIFTING THE STORY

1. *The Justice Syndicate*, direction and dramaturgy by Dan Barnard and Rachel Briscoe, Battersea Arts Centre, March 2019.

2. See Richard Philpot, Lasse Suonperä Liebst, Mark Levine, Wim Bernasco, and Marie Rosenkrantz Lindegaard, "Would I Be Helped? Cross-National CCTV Footage Shows That Intervention Is the Norm in Public Conflicts," *American Psychologist* 75, no. 1 (2020): 66–75; Charlotte Bloch, Lasse Suonperä Liebst, Poul Poder, Jasmin Maria

Christiansen, and Maria Bruvik Heinskou, "The Caring Collective and Other Forms of Bystander Help in Violent Situations," *Current Sociology* 66, no. 7 (2018): 1049–1069.

3. Sarah Maslin Nir and Arielle Dollinger, "Oceanside Stabbing: After a Brawl, Teenagers Gawked as Boy Lay Dying," *New York Times*, September 17, 2019.

4. Francesca Polletta, *It Was Like a Fever: Storytelling in Politics and Protest* (Chicago: University of Chicago Press, 2006).

5. David Olson, "Nassau Top Cop: Initial Reports of Teens at Oceanside Stabbing 'Misinterpreted,'" *Newsday*, September 25, 2019, https://www.newsday.com/long-island/nassau/oceanside-stabbing-video-morris-1.36805579.

6. See Joel Cooper, "Cognitive Dissonance," in *Social Psychology: Revisiting the Classic Studies*, ed. Joanne Smith and S. Alexander Haslam (London: Sage, 2012), 42–56.

7. Carol Travis and Eliot Aronson, *Mistakes Were Made (But Not by Me)* (Boston: Mariner Books, 2020), 22.

8. Leon Festinger, Henry Riecken, and Stanley Schachter, *When Prophecy Fails* (Mansfield, CT: Martino, 2011), 30.

9. Festinger, Riecken, and Schachter, 163.

10. Festinger, Riecken, and Schachter, 239–240.

11. Cooper, "Cognitive Dissonance," 42–56.

12. "Twelve Angry Men," *Studio One*, season 7, episode 1, directed by Franklin Schaffner, aired September 20, 1954, on CBS, https://www.youtube.com/watch?v=7DkI2IoW5i8.

13. Reginald Rose, *Twelve Angry Men*, ed. Stephen Price (London: Bloomsbury, 2016), 28.

14. Barnard and Briscoe, *Justice Syndicate*.

15. Dan Barnard and Kris De Meyer, "*The Justice Syndicate*: How Interactive Theatre Provides a Window into Jury Decision Making and the Public Understanding of the Law," *Law and Humanities*, September 2020, https://doi.org/10.1080/17521483.2020.1801137.

16. See the Innocence Project (2020), https://www.innocenceproject.org.

17. Saul Kassin, "False Confessions: Causes, Consequences, and Implications for Reform," *Policy Insights from the Behavioral and Brain Sciences* 1, no. 1 (2014): 112–121, https://doi.org/10.1177/2372732214548678.

18. Saul Kassin, "True or False: 'I'd Know a False Confession If I Saw One,'" *Law and Human Behavior* 29, no. 2 (April 2005): 211–227.

19. Alan Sekula, "On the Invention of Photographic Meaning," in *Thinking Photography*, ed. Burgin Victor (London: Palgrave, 1982).

20. Austin Sarat, Jessica Silbey, and Martha Merrill Umphrey, "Introduction: The Pleasures and Possibilities of Trial Films," in *Trial Films on Trial: Law, Justice and Popular Culture*, ed. Austin Sarat, Jessica Silbey and Martha Merrill Umphrey (Tuscaloosa: University of Alabama Press, 2019), 11.

21. Stanley Milgram Papers (SMP), Sterling Library, Yale University, box 75, folder 435.

22. SMP, box 75, folder 435.

23. SMP, box 75, folder 435.

24. Frederik Le Roy, "The Documentary Doubles of Milo Rau," *Theatre Times*, May 4, 2017, https://thetheatretimes.com/documentary-doubles-milo-rau/.

25. See N. Pennington and R. Hastie, "The Story Model for Juror Decision Making," in *Inside the Juror: The Psychology of Juror Decision Making*, ed. R. Hastie (Cambridge: Cambridge University Press, 1993), 191–221.

26. Evan Stark, *Coercive Control* (New York: Oxford University Press, 2009), 139.

27. Barnard and De Meyer, "*The Justice Syndicate*."

28. Louise Ellison and Vanessa Munro, "'Telling Tales': Exploring Narratives of Life and Law within the (Mock) Jury Room," *Legal Studies* 35, no. 2 (April 2015): 201–225.

29. Ellison and Munro, 220.

30. Ellison and Munro, 215.

31. Aida Rocci, "'The Justice Syndicate': How Do You Make Decisions: Immersive Theatre and Jury Duty," *Theatre Times*, February 27, 2019, https://thetheatretimes.com/the-justice-syndicate-how-do-you-make-decisions-immersive-theatre-and-jury-duty/.

32. Barnard and De Meyer, "*The Justice Syndicate*," 22.

33. Barnard and De Meyer, 32.

34. SMP, box 43, folder 24.

35. SMP, box 43, folder 129.

36. SMP, box 46, folder 164.

37. See Joanne Bernardi, "The Literary Link: Tanizaki and the Pure Film Movement," in *A Tanizaki Feast*, eds. Adriana Boscoro and Anthony Hood Chambers (Ann Arbor: University of Michigan Press, 1998), 79.

38. Salman Rushdie, *Haroun and the Sea of Stories* (London: Penguin, 2010), 72.

39. Arthur Frank, *Letting Stories Breathe: A Socio-Narratology* (Chicago: University of Chicago Press, 2010), 34.

40. Patrick Modiano, *Dora Bruder* (Berkeley: University of California Press, 2015), 56.

Index

"Obedience to Authority" (Milgram, 1963), 1, 53–54, 62, 100, 102; Abu Ghraib abuses compared with, 98; Asch's "Conformity and Independence" as basis of, 129; audiences for, 28, 36, 37; challenges to, 5, 105, 107; controversial ethics of, 75, 107, 111; experimental script for, 28; as "gold standard" of social psychology experiments, 104; Holocaust as influence, 41, 54; as "laboratory drama," 2, 26–29; mirrors used in, 28, 43, 48, 49; National Science Foundation funding for, 26, 131; "Pressure to Obey" version, 48, 52; refusal alongside obedience in, 23; screen adaptations of, 101; version 25 filmed, 4; Victim (Learner) role, 27, 28, 43, 45, 110, 111; "Women as Subjects" version, 110. See also Experimenter role; shock machine

"Obedience to Authority," participants in: families and descendants of, 50; "Gino Pasqual," 46; "Gretchen Brandt," 110–111; interviews with original participants, 103; Mr. and Mrs. 501, 40, 47–48, 49, 50–51, 52; New Haven City Council alderman, 48, 51, 52; New Haven private investigator, 50; public self-identification of, 50; shock machine unplugged by participant 20XX, 131; women, 40, 109–111, 112. See also "Prozi, Fred"

Obedience to Authority book (Milgram, 1974), 22, 37, 105

Open Theatre, 80

panoramas, 7
Paramount Pictures, 10, 11
Parella, Robert, 56
Parks, Gordon, 92
Pärt, Arvo, 52
patterns, 3, 22, 57
perceptions, 6, 10, 67, 124, 125
performance, 7, 122; of obedience and resistance, 31; of social actors, 35–36; verbatim, 110
Perry Mason (television series, 1957–1966), 43
persuasion techniques, 18
photography, 6, 7, 37–38, 130
Photo-Play, The: A Psychological Study (Münsterberg, 1916), 10
pictograph, 10
Piliavin, Irving, 4, 53, 61
Piliavin, Jane, 4, 53, 61, 63
Plantinga, Carl, 37, 38

police, 3, 43, 58, 60; "broken windows" theory and, 93; confessions induced by interrogation techniques, 126; Genovese murder investigation, 55, 56, 65; Gordon Parks photographs and, 92; real-life cops used in Stanford prison experiment, 69, 78; redacted police files, 122
police dramas, 46
Polish Laboratory Theatre, 79
Polletta, Francesca, 123
Prescott, Carlo, 71, 73, 76, 79, 119
Prirandello, Luigi, 80
prisoner-of-war movies, 45
"Prophecy from Another Planet" (*Lake City Herald*, 1954), 18–19
"Prozi, Fred," 22, 28–29, 138n20; "American Method" acting style and, 35, 36; as Everyman character, 38, 39; leading role as most obedient subject, 34; release form signed by, 39; unemployed condition as defining characteristic, 37
psychiatrists, 4, 41, 44, 45, 46, 48, 85; on bystander effect, 57; Genovese murder and, 57; portrayed in Hollywood movies, 51; in U.S. military, 15, 83; Yale University, 43
psychoanalysis, 12, 43
psychodrama, 79
Psychological Institute of Berlin, 14
psychology, 2, 4, 6; audiences for, 7; criminal, 46, 73; democratization of, 10; narrative, 5; observation methods, 12–15; role play in research and clinical contexts, 79; World War II as watershed moment in history of, 15; "yellow journalism" and, 11
"Psychology of Being Imprisoned, The" (Prescott seminar at Stanford), 71
Punishment Park (Watkins, 1971), 69–70, 80, 84–88, 86; newsreel quality of, 86–87; nonprofessional actors in, 87
purpose-built settings, 21, 73, 80; Gesell's photographic dome, 13; of the Gilbreths, 7; Milgram's Yale Interaction Laboratory, 27, 43, 73; in public locations, 73; Stanford prison experiment, 69, 73

race, bystander experiments and, 61, 63, 67
radio, 54, 63
Random 8 (Millard, 2011), 105
Rau, Milo, 127
realism, 61, 101, 105; historic specificity and, 107; hyperrealism, 106; Italian neorealist film, 103; poetic realism, 46

About the Author

KATHRYN MILLARD is a writer, independent filmmaker, and emeritus professor of screen and creative arts at Macquarie University, Sydney, Australia. Her body of screen work spans award-winning feature dramas, documentaries, and essay films. She is the author of *Screenwriting in a Digital Era*.